The *Fluent* READER

Oral & Silent Reading Strategies for Building Fluency, Word Recognition & Comprehension

Timothy V. Rasinski

SCHOLASTIC

New York • Toronto • London • Auckland • Sydney
Mexico City • New Delhi • Hong Kong • Buenos Aires

Cover design by Brian LaRossa
Cover photograph: ©Nico Hermann/Westend 61/Corbis
Interior design by Teresa B. Southwell
Interior photographs: Jean Schnell
Editor: Sarah Glasscock
Videographer: David Bourne/Bourne Media
Video editor: Maria Lilja

ISBN-13: 978-0-545-10836-2
ISBN-10: 0-545-10836-5

4 5 6 7 8 9 10   23   16 15 14 13 12 11

Contents

DVD

What's on the DVD

Video Clips
Conducting a Read Aloud
Antiphonal Reading
Choral Singing
Readers' Theater
A Reading Assessment

Ready-to-Print Pages
Forms
Paired Reading Record Sheet
Paired Reading Response Form
Repeated Reading Log
Cooperative Repeated Reading Response Form
Story Map
Lucky Listeners
Fast Start Parent Letter
Fast Start Reading Log
Word Recognition Error Form
Word Recognition Error Analysis Form
Multidimensional Fluency Scale Score Sheet

*Phrases and Short Sentences for
Repeated Reading Practice*

Texts for Practice and Performance
"Sojourner Truth and the Struggle for People's Equality"
"The Night Before Christmas"
"The Three Billy Goats Gruff (With Attitude!)"

Podcasts by Timothy V. Rasinski
Getting Started
In Conclusion

Acknowledgments

There are many people I wish to thank who have aided me, in one form or another, in the development of this book. First is Jerry Zutell from The Ohio State University, who guided me in my initial studies into reading fluency many years ago.

Thanks must also go to my colleagues and mentors at Kent State University, a wonderful place to learn about literacy and excellence in teaching literacy—in particular, Nancy Padak, Wendy Kasten, Belinda Zimmerman, Lori Wilfong, Richard Vacca, Karen Brothers, and the many other fantastic colleagues who have supported and enhanced my work in more ways than I can say.

Of course, I have many professional colleagues beyond Kent State who have been sources of knowledge, inspiration, insight, and encouragement who I need to recognize. These include, but certainly are not limited to, Dick Allington, Marie Biggs, Camille Blachowicz, Irene Blum, David Chard, Freddy Hiebert, Jim Hoffman, Susan Homan, Pat Koskinen, Melanie Kuhn, Kristin Lems, Wayne Linek, David Paige, Ray Reutzel, Jay Samuels, Paula Schwanenflugel, Steve Stahl, Betty Sturtevant, Bruce Stevenson, Stan Taylor, and Keith Topping. Thank you all.

I have also had the good fortune to work with fabulous classroom teachers, reading coaches, curriculum directors, and graduate students who have influenced deeply my thinking on oral reading and reading fluency. To Brenda Church, Gay Fawcett, Lorraine Griffith, Frances Imperator, Susan Johnston, Jodi Dodds Kinner, Lynne Kulich, Andy Rikli, Dana Solomon, Faith Wise, and Chase Young—to name just a few—go my deepest admiration and gratitude.

Although I have known and worked with Sarah Glasscock and Ray Coutu, my current and former editors on this book at Scholastic, for relatively brief periods of time, I am certainly indebted to both of them for their skillful and strategic advice and editing, as well as their cheerful and encouraging natures.

And finally I must thank my wife, Katherine Anne Rasinski, without whom neither this book nor any other book I have written or will ever write would be possible. Your enduring love and support truly sustain me. For that, I am truly blessed and sincerely grateful.

Dedication

I dedicate this book to my parents Laura and Chester Rasinski, my sister Charlotte, and my brother Richard, who taught me to read, not only through stories, but also through song, poetry, Mother Goose, jokes, letters, and prayer— texts that they read to me with fluency, passion, and meaning.

I also dedicate this book to the many knowledgeable and dedicated teachers I have met and worked with over the years who have shown and taught me the true meaning of reading fluency.

Foreword

Fluency, fluency, fluency! Unlike years ago when fluency was the most neglected aspect of reading instruction, today it seems that fluency has assumed a position of such prominence that many are describing it somewhat disparagingly as the age of DIBELS (Dynamic Indicators of Basic Early Literacy Skills). It is difficult to visit a contemporary classroom to observe reading instruction where fluency practice has not assumed a fairly central role and a significant portion of the allocated instructional time. Children and teachers can now speak "fluency-ese," referring quite naturally to real and nonsense words, words correct per minute, DIBELS tests and benchmarks, etc. In fact, I was in one very effective second-grade teacher's classroom in a local Reading First project two years ago where the teacher had prepared a folder on which students recorded their words correct per minute (wcpm) on a personal graph every two weeks. The graph had a blue line drawn between each student's first-of-the-year wcpm timing and the grade-level goal at the end of the year—referred to as the grade-level fluency trajectory line. One student had just completed his two-week timing to record in his folder. Each two-week point on the graph was connected with a red line showing his gradual increase in reading rate. But today, I observed for the first time that his reading timing red line had crossed the blue grade-level fluency trajectory line. Having recorded this banner event, the student's response was quite instructive. "Wow," said he. "I had better slow down!"

This snippet from the classroom typifies what I believe too many teachers and students have come to think about fluency practice and instruction. The sum total of the game has become largely to increase reading rate! I do not place the blame on a much vilified inanimate object—DIBELS. Like any other tool, DIBELS is just that—an assessment tool. How DIBELS is used and abused is largely the product of human understanding and behavior. DIBELS as an indicator suggests that if decoding is going along somewhat automatically and effortlessly, then the possibility for cognitive attention to be allocated to comprehension is more likely to occur. There are few researchers or practitioners, I believe, who would quarrel long with the assertion that decoding makes comprehension more likely to occur.

The truly unfortunate outcome of using DIBELS, as a tool, has been the use of this tool to craft a de facto and reductionist definition of fluency—a rate attenuated by accuracy. I, like others, worry about how the definition of fluency has become distorted by the use of DIBELS for something more than a progress-monitoring assessment. If students are reading too slowly, what does this mean? Does it mean we should place them in an intervention that encourages them to read more rapidly? DIBELS is not a diagnostic assessment, nor was it ever represented as such. DIBELS was never intended to be used as a practical definition of fluency, but it has unwittingly contributed to such a state of affairs! Fluency without comprehension, as Jay Samuels has rightly pointed out, is NOT fluency. I believe most classroom teachers would never say a student is a fluent reader if he or she could not comprehend what was read; but this broader, comprehensive view of the fluent reader is being obscured in today's frenzied efforts to increase DIBELS scores.

So while moving fluency onto the center stage of reading instruction is and has been a long-awaited, positive development in reading instruction, it has also raised many concerns, questions, and issues relative to fluency assessment, instruction, and practice. Let me enumerate just a few.

I have yet to observe fluency assessments or instructional interventions in classrooms that give appropriate attention to the reader's executive or meta-cognitive control of accuracy, rate, and expression for a variety of purposes and across a variety of text difficulty levels and types. While rate is a relatively good indicator of whether or not a reader can decode with ease, rate is also strongly influenced by a "fluent" reader's vocabulary and comprehension of a text. The lack of sensitive assessments and instructional interventions that give appropriate focus to developing within readers executive control of fluency processes, or "meta-fluency," represents a contemporary negligence in fluency instruction akin to that which Richard Allington noted about fluency generally in decades past. Students need to understand that they can and must take active, intentional control of the elements of fluency—accuracy, rate, and expression—to the end of comprehending what they read to become truly fluent readers.

A second issue related to fluency is the mind-numbing practice of oral repeated readings with texts that contain little knowledge of consequence or fail to present students with aesthetically engaging content. The quality of texts for practice is an area ripe for research and improvements in classroom fluency instructional practices.

A third issue relates to how norms were established for benchmarking student oral reading rates at grade level. In most cases, such oral reading rate norms were obtained by using grade-level texts read for a single minute. This assessment approach begs several questions. Would oral reading rates be different for different genres, text types, or text difficulty levels? If so, how would these variations affect oral reading norms? What about the issue of reading stamina? Current oral reading rates represent reading "sprint" rates of a single minute. Do oral reading rates decrease when reading texts for longer periods of time? And then there is the question of silent reading rates. How can we measure these efficiently and effectively to understand the relationship between oral and silent reading rates and how to help children transition from their highly developed oral reading skills to silent reading? There are many more examples that I could surface for discussion, but the point here is to introduce the second edition of Tim Rasinski's enormously popular and useful book, *The Fluent Reader*.

From the moment *The Fluent Reader* first appeared in 2003, it quickly became the quintessential book on fluency for classroom teachers. Readers soon found that Dr. Rasinski had artfully woven a tapestry of research and practice about reading fluency that made both equally accessible. Tim is a master teacher and a recognized researcher who brings theory, research, and practice together into an extremely readable new edition of *The Fluent Reader*.

In this new edition, Tim reviews the history of oral reading and the methods that were used to perpetuate generations of "round robin" reading practice, a classroom practice that has been found to be detrimental to students primarily because of the way in which individual student practice time is constrained when students wait to practice reading until their turn comes around. Even popular methods such as "popcorn" reading in many ways work to constrain students' engagement in reading. Throughout this new edition, Tim provides readers with an update on fluency research that has occurred during the past decade, the most research-productive historic period of reading fluency research! When Tim recommends a practice to increase fluency, teachers can rely on the fact that there is empirical, classroom-tested evidence that such a practice results in real improvements in engagement and reading practice that promotes fluent reading.

I am so impressed with Dr. Rasinski's voice in this edition. He writes in a style and manner that is inviting and personal. As a reader, you feel as if you are with a helpful colleague who wants very much to help you offer your students exceptional reading fluency instruction and practice. Tim never loses sight of the golden ring of fluency—student comprehension and motivation. He makes clear that fluency practice that fails to engage students' minds and hearts will not motivate students to persist in doing the work to understand challenging texts and ideas. He reminds us that fluency is not fluent reading when students do not read a variety of high-quality texts for clearly articulated purposes.

Tim also reminds us of the power of performance to motivate effective fluency practice. The relevance of reading practice is greatly heightened when students know that they will perform their reading for an audience. In this second edition of *The Fluent Reader*, Tim stresses the research-proven value of performances such as readers' theater, radio reading, and recitations.

I particularly appreciate Tim's attention to developing the language of "meta-fluency" with students. In this edition, he reiterates the importance of helping students acquire the language of fluency and the active mental-control processes that fluent readers employ when reading a variety of texts for differing purposes. If one is searching for information, scanning or skimming is appropriate. Stopping and musing over shared experiences in a well-crafted story to make personal connections is part of reading for enjoyment. Fluent readers slow down to study the intricacies of a diagram in an information text on amphibian life cycles. A moving poem or an entertaining joke promotes students' willingness to practice a text again and again to commit the text to memory. Students need to understand that fluent reading is not always about rushing through texts, but knowing when to consciously take control of reading rate for a variety of texts and purposes.

Another hallmark of this new edition is a presentation on how to expand the assessment of fluency beyond the simplistic measurement of accuracy and rate to include aspects of expression such as pacing, smoothness, volume, expression, phrasing, etc. Tim also repeats the cautions about current reading fluency assessments that narrow the focus of reading fluency instruction and practice to decoding and fail to direct sufficient attention to the end goal—facilitation of reading comprehension and student engagement. In this edition, Tim expands his discussion of a variety of ways to comprehensively assess students' fluency growth over time.

Tim has established himself as one of the nation's foremost leaders in reading fluency. His contributions to research and practice have been published in prestigious journals, book chapters, and books. He presents regularly at the International Reading Association, National Reading Conference, and the College Reading Association/Association of Literacy Educators & Researchers. He is a curious, avid learner who is genuinely a student of how reading fluency is acquired and to what ends. He has been the one to ask us all to pay attention to the thorny issues in reading fluency instruction and practice. As such, he constantly reminds us all of what we know, what we need to know, and why we need to know it when it comes to reading fluency.

I have had the privilege of working with Tim over the years in a variety of professional organizations and on several interesting and challenging writing projects, including the first chapter ever to be published exclusively on reading fluency in the fourth edition of the *Handbook of Reading Research*. Tim is a teacher's teacher. He is one of the kindest and most genuinely caring members of the reading profession. He cares deeply about teachers and children, schools and administrators, programs and people. I am fortunate enough to count him as a friend and a mentor.

In this new edition, Dr. Tim Rasinski provides a richly illustrated guidebook for teachers who are searching for ways to take fluency instruction and practice from the mundane to the motivating and from the mechanical to the artful. All along the way in this new edition, you the teacher will find rich ideas for exciting and memorable texts, motivating and effective teaching practices, and comprehensive fluency assessments. Tim moves us all beyond the narrow landscape of today's DIBELS fluency world of assessment and practice, to that of a thoughtful consideration of the issues, forward-looking solutions to today's problems, and expansive assessment options that truly embrace all that we mean by the term . . . *The Fluent Reader*.

D. Ray Reutzel
Emma Eccles Jones Distinguished Professor
Emma Eccles Jones Center for Early Childhood Education
Department of Teacher Education and Leadership
Utah State University, Logan, Utah

Introduction

Oral reading holds a rather enigmatic place in America's classrooms. And it's easy to see why when we look back on its history. In the nineteenth century, oral reading dominated reading instruction in the United States. However, at the beginning of the twentieth century, it was largely and vociferously shunned by most reading scholars, and its popularity began to wane. Even today, at the beginning of the twenty-first century, some reading educators believe that oral reading should play, at best, a limited role in beginning reading instruction and in diagnosing reading problems. Their goal is to move students toward silent reading, the most common form of reading for most adults, as quickly as possible. Moreover, despite these educators' views, many teachers at all grade levels practice a detrimental form of oral reading daily: round robin reading.

Current, research-based forms of oral reading instruction, forms other than round robin reading, deserve a legitimate, primary, and integral place in the reading curriculum at every grade level and for students of all levels of achievement. Of course, silent reading should take on a more prominent role as students move up the grades. However, oral reading should continue to play a prominent role as well, because it leads to better silent reading and because oral reading is part and parcel of the literate lives of all readers. We use oral reading in many ways, naturally in the real world, outside the classroom. For example, we find oral reading every time we turn on the television or radio and listen to the news. We see the fruits of oral reading every time we attend a play. We read orally whenever we sing or pray in our places of worship. We read orally when we read to our children every night. Indeed, my wife and I read to each other quite often—books, news articles, letters from friends. Truly, the key goals of the school reading program, most notably reading fluency (but also phonics, or word recognition, and reading comprehension) can be achieved effectively through oral reading.

Many teachers I speak with want to weave more progressive and effective forms of oral reading into their curriculum but don't have the tools or the knowledge to do so, which comes as no surprise. Take a look at almost any reading methods textbook for the elementary grades and you will find a dearth of information on using oral reading for instructional purposes. In one of today's most popular textbooks, for example, fewer than 5 of its 600 pages are devoted to oral reading. Because silent reading has become such a dominant form of literacy in the world, oral reading, unfortunately, is often viewed as something to be avoided as much as possible in the classroom.

This book is meant to fill that gap by increasing teachers' knowledge of oral reading fluency and providing ways to make oral reading and fluency instruction an effective and integral part of a balanced reading program. In this book, I provide a brief overview of the history, advantages, and general uses of oral reading and fluency. From there, the book offers a variety of effective strategies for employing oral reading in enjoyable and engaging ways, providing evidence, where available, for their effectiveness.

Knowledge is power. My hope in writing this book is that sound knowledge of oral reading instruction will lead you to more effective instruction for all your students.

The DVD accompanying this edition contains podcasts by Timothy Rasinski and video clips showing a read aloud, antiphonal reading, choral singing, readers' theater, and a reading assessment in action. You'll also find ready-to-print PDFs of all the forms and word lists in this book.

Chapter 1

Overview of Oral Reading and Reading Fluency

A Brief History and Rationale

". . . I would suggest that our idea of reading is incomplete, impoverished, unless we are also taking the time to read aloud."

—Verlyn Klinkenborg
Editorial Board, *New York Times*
May 16, 2009

Step into any elementary or middle school classroom around the world and you are likely to see oral reading at some point in the day. Perhaps the teacher is reading aloud a favorite book. Maybe the entire class is reading together a poem or song lyric printed on a chart. Perhaps individual students are reading silently, but because the text is a bit challenging, you notice them subvocalizing as they read. You might see pairs of students nestled in corners and nooks throughout their classroom, reading to each other. You're also likely to find small and large groups of students reading a single text together—one student is called on by the teacher to read orally while the other students follow along silently. After a few minutes, the teacher calls on another student to read orally. The routine continues until the passage is completed.

No matter how you feel about oral reading, it is a common feature in classrooms around the globe. Teachers find it a useful instructional tool. This book explores the nature of oral reading and powerful ways to weave it into the curriculum—especially to develop reading fluency, a key component of proficient reading. But first, let's look at the history of oral reading in the United States. If you use or intend to use oral reading in your classroom, it is wise to understand how it became such a pervasive part of elementary and middle school education. Knowing our past helps us understand our present and, perhaps, chart the future of oral reading in an informed way.

▶The Earliest Days of Oral Reading Instruction

Oral reading has a rich history in the homes and classrooms of the United States. In the days prior to iPhones, iPods, PDAs, computers, television, and radio, reading was a primary form of family entertainment and information sharing. However, according to reading historians (Hyatt, 1943; Smith, 1965), in many early American homes books were scarce and usually only one person could read. Therefore, for all family members to benefit from texts, that one person had to read selections aloud. Because of its prominence in daily life, oral reading was the focus of classroom instruction (Hyatt, 1943).

From the earliest days of the United States through the first decade of the twentieth century, oral reading dominated school instruction. In fact, some schools were called "blab schools" because students were required to read orally, reread, and memorize their lessons. They simultaneously read assigned texts orally—often texts that were different from what their classmates were assigned.

The cacophony of voices must have been quite disquieting, to say the least! On other occasions, students read chorally one text written on the chalkboard. When you imagine what those schools must have looked like or—more appropriately—sounded like, it's clear the term "blab school" fit.

By the middle of the nineteenth century, textbooks were used in many classrooms for reading instruction, especially for oral reading instruction. The passages that follow are from textbooks by two popular authors of the time, William Holmes McGuffey and M. A. Newell. Notice the emphasis they place on word decoding, recitation, and elocution.

> *"In this book, all new words in each lesson are given at the head of the lesson. The pupil should be able to identify these words at sight, and to pronounce them correctly, before reading aloud the sentences in which they occur."*   —McGuffey, 1887

> *"Thorough and frequent drill on the elementary sounds is useful in correcting vicious habits of pronunciation, and in strengthening the vocal organs."*   —McGuffey, 1879a

> *"Drills in articulations and emphasis should be given with every lesson. The essentials of good reading are not to be taught by one or two lessons. Constant drill on good exercises, with frequent exhibitions of the correct method from the teacher, will be found more effectual than any form prescribed in type."*   —McGuffey, 1879b

> *"All reading drills are best managed by concert recitations; but reading for individual practice should not be supplanted by simultaneous reading."*
> —Newell, 1880

The development of "eloquent oral reading" became the aim of reading instruction in this period (Smith, 1965). Many authors of reading texts identified the goal of reading instruction as Lyman Cobb and David Tower do here:

> *"A just delivery consists in a distinct articulation of words pronounced in proper tones, suitably varied to the sense, and the emotions of the mind;*

with due attention to accent, to emphasis, in its several gradations; to rests or pauses of the voice, in proper places . . . and the whole accompanied with expressive looks, and significant gestures. . . . That the pupil may be assisted in forming a correct method of reading and speaking, a few rules shall be laid down, pointing out a proper use of each of those necessary parts of a just delivery."   —Lyman Cobb, cited in Smith, 1965

"Correct articulation is the basis of this art [reading], and we must look well to the foundation before we can safely raise the superstructure; it is, therefore, necessary that, in the order of teaching, it should take precedence. . . ."   —David Tower, cited in Smith, 1965

Teachers began to use a form of oral recitation that focused on elocution or correct pronunciation (Hoffman & Segel, 1983; Hoffman, 1987). Lessons involved the teacher reading a text orally—usually a story, but sometimes a fable, poem, or prayer—followed by students practicing the text orally on their own. Often the teacher would provide assistance and evaluation of the individual student's reading. Then, after a sufficient period of practice, the students would recite the text for the teacher and fellow students. The students' reading was judged on the quality of their oral reading and their recall of what they had read. According to Hoffman (1987), this approach to reading instruction became formalized at the beginning of the twentieth century into what was called the "story method" of instruction, since the focal unit of instruction was an entire text or fully contained passage. Advocates of the story method often used the classic texts of the time, such as "The Tortoise and the Hare," "The Fox and the Hound," and poetry by Tennyson, Scott, and Stevenson (Smith, 1965).

By the latter half of the nineteenth century, oral reading had become such an ingrained and seemingly necessary part of American education that philosopher William James (1892, as cited in Hoffman & Segel, 1983) indicated that "the teacher's success or failure in teaching reading is based, so far as the public estimate is concerned, upon the oral reading method."

➤ Oral Reading in Decline

Near the end of the nineteenth and the beginning of the twentieth centuries, oral reading's popularity as the primary mode of instruction began to wane.

European and American education scholars began to question the effectiveness of oral reading instruction in American classrooms (Hyatt, 1943), arguing that it gave priority to elocutionary matters such as "pronunciation, emphasis, inflection, and force" (Hyatt, 1943, p. 27) over reading for understanding. Horace Mann (1891), for example, claimed that reading instruction had become more an "action of the organs of speech" rather than an "exercise of the mind in thinking and feeling," and that "more than eleven-twelfths of all the children in reading classes do not understand the meaning for the words they read."

Similarly, Francis Parker, who is often associated with the language experience approach (LEA) to reading instruction, began to question the use of oral reading for instructional purposes, based on the educational theories of Friedrich Froebel in Germany (Hyatt, 1943). He argued that oral reading in schools placed inappropriate emphasis on elocution over understanding:

> *"Many of the grossest errors in teaching reading spring from confounding the two processes of attention and expression. Reading itself is not expression. . . . Reading is a mental process. . . . Oral reading is expression, and comes under the heading of speech. . . . The custom of making oral reading the principal and almost the only means of teaching reading has led to many errors prevalent to-day."*   (Parker, 1884)

The Shift to Silent Reading

Behavioral science began to have an impact on reading education near the beginning of the twentieth century. Some reading scholars, such as Edmund Huey, noted that reading orally had become a task that was found only in schools, while in everyday life, silent reading predominated. Huey wrote:

> *"Reading as a school exercise has almost always been thought of as reading aloud, in spite of the obvious fact that reading in actual life is to be mainly silent reading. . . . The consequent attention to reading as an exercise in speaking, and it has usually been a rather bad exercise in speaking at that, has been heavily at the expense of reading as the art of thought-getting and thought manipulating. . . . By silent reading meanings*

from the first day of reading, and by practice in getting meanings from the page . . . the rate of reading and of thinking will grow with the pupil's growth and with his power to assimilate what is read." (Huey, 1908)

The focus on abstracting meaning from text over oral production of the text began to take hold. And silent reading became the primary vehicle for teaching comprehension among students.

During this time, scientists were attempting to identify and study the basic components of their fields of study. Chemists and physicists were studying essential elements of nature, for example. Biologists were studying the cell and its components. And, for many educational psychologists who were studying reading, the word became the basic component. These reading scholars looked at the frequency of words in texts, as well as the decodability of those words (i.e., how easily words could be decoded or "sounded out"). As a result, researchers created texts for instructional purposes made up of a large number of high-frequency and easily decodable words. The theory held that students would read these words in texts repeatedly and, in the process, the words would become part of their sight vocabulary (i.e., words recognized instantly by the reader upon encountering them in the text). Of course, those texts often sounded contrived, were less than interesting, and were not at all authentic.

The Impact of an Increase in Print Material

During this period, the number of books, magazines, newspapers, and other materials available to adults and children began to expand at a rapid pace (Hyatt, 1943). For students and teachers to take advantage of and cover this growing body of print, silent reading, which was inherently quicker and more efficient than oral reading, needed to be emphasized. In their series of instructional reading books, Buswell and Wheeler (1923) noted that schools that employed oral reading used very few readers or other forms of reading materials.

"In contrast with this, in the modern school, which emphasizes silent reading, a great many books are read in each grade. . . . It [silent reading] is the complex process of getting thought from printed page and involves an entirely new pedagogy. Silent-reading objectives will never be attained by oral-reading methods."

Moreover, as reading material became more accessible, the need for oral reading for imparting information at home and in the community declined. Individual silent reading became more common in family and community life.

A Change in Reading Instruction

Silent reading began to replace oral reading as the preferred mode of reading instruction. Scholars felt that silent reading was a more authentic form of reading because, for most readers in the real world, it was more common than oral reading. Silent reading focused readers' attention on grasping meaning—the ultimate goal of reading—while oral reading tended to focus attention on the accurate pronunciation of words and the recitation of text. Scholars also felt that silent reading maximized the number of texts students read and that students were more likely to understand a text upon their first and only silent reading of it, thus increasing the opportunity for them to read many texts; oral reading instruction, on the other hand, aimed at expressiveness in reading through intensive practice of a limited number of texts (Hoffman & Segel, 1983). Moreover, in oral recitation reading activities, only one student read at a time, while the remaining students listened. As such, reading volume was limited. Silent reading, on the other hand, could easily be done by multiple students simultaneously.

The Indianapolis Public Schools' *Course of Study in Reading* for 1902 had this to say about reading instruction:

> *"Reading . . . fundamentally is not oral expression. Children should do as much silent reading and be called upon to state the salient features of such reading in order to know how far they have grasped the thought. Silent reading is too much neglected in schools. . . . Pupils should be taught how to read silently with the greatest economy of time and with the least conscious effort."*

By the 1920s, silent reading was entrenched in American schools. The following item from the Course of Study series from the Ohio Department of Education (State of Ohio, 1923) reflects this fundamental change:

> *"During the past few years investigations have been in progress along several lines in reading, one of the most important having to do with the significant*

factors in silent reading and the emphasis due this type. It would be amiss not to suggest here some of the values of training in silent reading:

1. *It is the most economical form of reading.*
2. *Silent reading bears a close relationship to the other school subjects in that attainment in other subjects depends largely upon ability to read.*
3. *Training in silent reading constitutes a real preparation for life reading.*
4. *Silent reading develops interest because thought plays a prominent part."*

According to Nila Banton Smith (1965), schools almost became obsessed with the notion of silent reading for improving comprehension and reading speed. In fact, from the 1930s through the early 1940s, Chicago schools adopted a program, called the "non-oral method," that emphasized the teaching of silent reading exclusively. Followers taught students to gain meaning directly from printed symbols by using only their eyes and central nervous system, and no inner speech (McDade, 1937, 1944; Rohrer, 1943). Students could not make oral representations of words. Even silent reading that involved internal sounding out of words was discouraged. Although severely criticized (Rohrer, 1943) and eventually abandoned, the emergence of the "non-oral" method demonstrates the extent to which oral reading, and by default reading fluency, was viewed as unnecessary and, in some cases, detrimental to success in learning to read. Indeed, the de-emphasis of oral reading for instruction left assessment as the primary purpose for oral reading.

"With the shift from oral reading of authentic stories to silent reading of contrived texts that stressed particular words and word features, oral reading took on at best a secondary role in the reading classroom. It [oral reading] was used primarily to check students' word recognition after silent reading. This was the genesis of round robin reading, or turn-taking reading, which was integrated in a minor way into the basal reading programs that assumed a preeminent position in elementary reading instruction from the early 1950s to the present" (Hoffman, 1987).

➤ The Rise of Round Robin Reading

Round robin reading, the long-standing method in which the teacher calls on students one by one to read orally, began as a way to assess students' ability to decode words. A student would read orally for the teacher who, rather than coaching the student on his or her performance, would check for errors in the performance. In some ways, it was like administering the oral reading portion of an informal reading inventory or a running record today. Students were given additional instruction in the words they missed or on any word patterns they had difficulty reading.

When round robin reading was done in a group, it offered the teacher advantages beyond assessing students' reading. It gave the teacher control over the group because he or she could call on a student to read without warning, after another student had read. Because the teacher did not assign portions of the text in advance, each student had to follow along silently while a classmate read orally so that he or she could pick up the reading if asked. Round robin reading required minimal preparation as well—the teacher just had to pick a passage and a reader. If a student missed a word, the teacher would either guide him or her in decoding it or, more commonly, simply give the correct pronunciation and move on. In addition to making life easier for the teacher, round robin reading made students' reading proficiency a public matter and, thus, in the view of many, motivating the less proficient reader to work harder.

Clearly, round robin reading found favor with many teachers. To this day, it continues to be practiced in all grades and with students at all levels of achievement. Indeed, Hoffman (1987) noted that in nearly every classroom he visited during a study of reading instruction, he observed round robin reading taking place—usually with little or no preparation for reading the passage and no discussion of the passage after the reading. Hoffman's observations mirror my own, and probably those of anyone else who has observed reading instruction in the United States over the last 50 years. Round robin reading continues to be an embedded and ubiquitous part of classroom culture in the United States.

Drawbacks of Round Robin Reading

Despite its widespread use, round robin reading has never been widely advocated nor endorsed by scholars of reading. For example, Eldredge, Reutzel, and Hollingsworth (1996) found that it was inferior to the shared book experience, another form of instructional book reading, in promoting word recognition accuracy, fluency, vocabulary acquisition, and comprehension. During a round robin reading session, one student reads orally at a time. Ideally, while that student reads, the other students follow along silently in their books. This is typically not the case, however. Knowing that they will be called upon during the lesson, students often look ahead to scout out what they might be asked to read. The teacher, facing the double and daunting task of instructing the student who's reading while keeping the rest of the group's attention on the text (Hoffman, 1987), may choose to call on the next student at an unanticipated point in the text. Students and teacher end up playing a game of sorts (and not a very productive one at that) during a round robin reading lesson. Students try to predict what they will be asked to read, while the teacher "surprises" them by calling on them to read at unanticipated times and locations in the text. When this happens, the student often does not know where to begin reading and must be told, which can be embarrassing.

For some students, oral reading—particularly when it is not rehearsed—can be challenging. They may not read with a great deal of fluency or expression. They may miss words and have to be given the correct pronunciation by the teacher or another student. Many students find this public display of disfluent reading an embarrassment that they never forget. And it's not only the reader who suffers. The other group members—the students who must listen to a slow, labored, and error-filled reading—may become bored with and distracted from the text.

Round robin reading's drawbacks have been recognized by teachers and scholars for years (Opitz & Rasinski, 2008). So why do teachers continue to practice it? The answer lies in the fact that teachers have not been given many viable alternatives (Hoffman, 1987). Indeed, in many teacher education classes, the only alternative to such traditional forms of oral reading is silent reading. Without more progressive forms of oral reading, silent reading is given primacy in elementary classrooms by default or oral reading is simply not an option.

➤ Why Oral Reading in the Twenty-First Century? A Rationale

The fact of the matter is that oral reading is not dead in elementary and middle school classrooms, nor should it be. High-quality forms of oral reading, which I describe later, play an important role in reading education and should be an integral and complementary part of any program, along with silent reading. Indeed, at least one study has linked student oral reading at home with higher overall reading achievement (Postlethwaite & Ross, 1992). In the university reading clinic where I work with struggling readers and supervise teachers who instruct them, oral reading is an important part of our teaching. We find that students respond well to the strategies we employ and make solid gains in their reading achievement. In this section, I outline key reasons why oral reading should have an esteemed place in elementary and middle school classrooms.

Oral Reading Can Be a Fun, Engaging, and Authentic Experience

Oral reading can be an enjoyable experience. Most students love to hear their teachers read aloud the very best trade books, for example. Listening to an expressive and meaning-filled voice can draw students into the magic of reading.

In the graduate and undergraduate courses I teach, I often ask students to describe some of their most memorable moments in learning to read. Without question, their number-one answer is being read to—by a parent, a grandparent, a sibling, a primary-grade teacher, or other adult. Reading aloud at home and school was an authentic and valued part of family and classroom life. Sometimes, students report memories of being read to by a middle or high school teacher. These instances might be rare, but they are also among the most memorable and most enriching reading experiences of my adult students.

In a study of middle school students, Gay Ivey and Karen Broaddus (2001) surveyed nearly 2,000 sixth graders about their interests in reading and reading instruction. The number-one reading activity mentioned by students was free reading time. They appreciated the opportunity to read silently materials of their own choosing. However, very close behind free reading time was read-aloud time.

Sixty-two percent of students indicated a love of being read to by their teacher. Even older students recognized the motivational power of being read to—it made them want to read more on their own.

How Read Aloud Benefits Students

"Mr. Leonard reads to us every day after lunch. He is a really good reader. He does the voice really cool. It just makes it fun . . . how he does the voices usually makes it funny like when he says something or if something funny happens because sometimes he starts laughing in the middle while he's reading." — *Katherine*, sixth grader

"He reads all kinds of books. I think he's kind of feeling like he's read all of them previously, and then if he likes them, he reads them to us. Listen to him. I like how Mr. Leonard—he'll change his voice for all the characters. It makes it easier to follow who everybody is." — *Matthew*, sixth grader

(Ivey & Broaddus, 2001, p. 360)

Katherine and Matthew capture the magic inherent in read aloud. Specifically, students:

- **see reading as emotionally and aesthetically powerful.** By reading aloud to students, teachers model their own delight in books, that aesthetic or affective response that Louise Rosenblatt (1978) says is an essential to the reading experience. Although many teachers are embarrassed when a book brings them to tears, they read to their students anyway. And often their students themselves are moved to find that a story can have such an impact on an adult.
- **are motivated to read more.** Teachers read to students to instill in them a love of reading. A large international study conducted by Postlethwaite and Ross found that when

teachers encouraged their students to read, they realized higher student achievement in reading (Postlethwaite & Ross, 1992). The researchers also found a direct relationship between encouragement, motivation, and reading achievement. Students who were encouraged to read, read more and at higher levels of achievement than students who were not. Postlethwaite and Ross also found that the amount of reading students did in school and at home was strongly associated with high achievement.

- **witness fluent reading.** By reading aloud with expression, teachers model for students meaningful, fluent reading. Many students believe that good reading is word-perfect, accurate decoding. Although this is important, it is the expressive reading by the teacher that makes read aloud so special. Students learn that, to have the same impact when they read aloud, they need to read with expression. And, as Matthew perceptively suggests, the way to achieve that is to practice the text before reading it aloud.

- **are exposed to multiple genres.** Teachers often use read aloud to share genres that students may not normally pick up on their own (Huck, 1977). In doing so, teachers stretch students' minds by exposing them to reading materials with which they may not be familiar.

- **explore sophisticated words and text structures.** Teachers can read aloud material that is above students' own reading level. This provides rich language stimulation by exposing students to more sophisticated vocabulary and sentence structures (Cazden, 1972). As a result, students' word knowledge and comprehension skills improve. (For more on read aloud, see Chapter 2.)

In the Ivey and Broaddus (2001) study, another type of oral reading was popular: reading plays and poetry out loud. Most people want to be recognized for their talents. However, to be recognized, they must display those talents. To be recognized as a reader of poetry or prose, or as an actor, we need to read aloud. Over a third of students in the survey indicated that they most enjoyed reading aloud for performance.

When we give students opportunities to practice a play or poem beforehand, it is nearly impossible for them to fail. Whether they are putting on a play, performing a readers' theater script, or reading a poem in the weekly class coffeehouse, reading aloud for performance can make anyone feel like a star. (For more on performance reading, see Chapter 5.)

Oral Reading Is Real Reading and Real Language

Oral reading in classrooms is often dismissed because it is not viewed as an authentic or "real" form of reading. Critics say that because adults read silently more frequently than they do orally, children do not need oral reading instruction in school. While silent reading may be more common in our society, it is grossly inaccurate to say that we don't use oral reading in authentic, everyday ways. The many occasions for it include the following:

- Reading stories (usually by a teacher or parent)
- Reciting poetry
- Performing scripts, dialogues, and monologues
- Giving speeches
- Singing songs
- Announcing public proclamations and pledges
- Sharing letters, notes, and personal communications
- Offering toasts
- Reporting news
- Telling jokes
- Shouting cheers

Stories, poems, scripts, speeches, and other text forms are meant to be read or performed aloud. Any reading program worth its salt should contain a wide variety of texts for students to explore. Reading poetry and singing song lyrics offer students the opportunity to read what poet Robert Pinsky calls "reciting rhythmical words [meant to be read] aloud." These texts allow students to develop a love of and appreciation for this wonderful and powerful language we call English. Thus, texts like these, and more, need to be part of a reading program—whether that program is developed by a publishing company or teachers. And reading these types of texts orally should be a natural part of the program.

Oral Reading Builds Confidence

Many young people lack confidence in themselves as readers. This is evident in the university reading clinic where I supervise teachers who work with struggling students. Because of their poor reading skills, these students don't often view themselves as successful or even potentially successful readers. When we ask them to read orally for assessment purposes, these students hunch their bodies, bow their heads, move their faces close to the text, and read in a barely audible voice. Certainly, children who read this way do not think much of themselves as learners.

Oral reading performance has the potential to transform a self-conscious student into a star performer—especially when he or she is coached and given opportunities to practice. We often see this most clearly on the last day of our reading clinic's term. Children who entered the program timid and shy step up and perform confidently for their families a poem, script, or other text that they have been working on over the final few days. These children have been transformed—not only as readers and learners, but also as people. Oral reading is the vehicle that allows them to find their voices.

The confidence-building potential of oral reading is evident in the journal comments of second graders who participated in a three-month study of oral reading performance. One of these students, Lucia, wrote, "I never thought I could be a star, but I was the best reader today" (Martinez, Roser, & Strecker, 1999).

Oral Reading Creates Community

Reading is often viewed as a solitary act, particularly when students read in silence. But reading can easily be used to build community among students, particularly when they engage in oral reading. When students read in a choral fashion, for example, they implicitly say to one another that they are part of a classroom community. If the text is the Pledge of Allegiance or a patriotic song, that community may reach beyond the classroom to encompass their fellow citizens, perhaps all of society.

Similarly, when older and younger students are paired up for cross-grade reading, friendships can form that reach beyond the classroom. Even within the classroom, when students pair up with peers, or when one student reads to a larger group of peers, a connection develops between the reader and the audience.

Oral Reading Connects Spoken and Written Language

The language experience approach (Stauffer, 1980) helps students see the connection between their oral speech and written words. To carry out this approach, a common experience, such as a field trip, is shared by a group of students, discussed in class, and then transferred into print, with the teacher as scribe. The teacher then shows students that the process of encoding speech can also be reversed, by decoding the words she's just written into speech—in other words, through oral reading. Through this regular process of encoding and decoding, students recognize the organic connection between speaking and listening, and writing and reading. Reading may not seem so difficult or distant to students when seen through the lens of the language experience approach.

Oral Reading Strengthens Decoding Skills

Decoding skills are often taught using words in isolation. Students are taught to examine words carefully to identify them or sound them out accurately. Most proponents of word recognition instruction argue that studying words in isolation must be balanced with studying them within the context of reading. While silent reading should certainly be part of the mix in developing word recognition skills, so should oral reading.

Many theories claim that learning is most effective when a maximum number of senses or sensory modalities are involved. For example, the motor theory of learning, which suggests that bodily movement can facilitate learning (Block, Parris, & Whiteley, 2008; Hoffman, 1991; Washburn, 1914), has been around a long time and is implied in Howard Gardner's (1983) more recent theory of multiple intelligences, which suggests that the learning that normally occurs in one intelligence can be facilitated through the application of other intelligences.

Multisensory approaches to word learning have been advocated for years as well. One such approach is the kinesthetic approach, or VAKT (visual, auditory, kinesthetic, tactile), where students learn to decode words by simultaneously looking at the word to be learned, saying and hearing the word, touching it, and tracing it (Harris & Sipay, 1990). There are many well-documented reports of the kinesthetic approach's success with students who have severe difficulties in learning (Kress & Johnson, 1970; Myers, 1978). The kinesthetic and auditory aspects of oral reading, then, can reinforce and facilitate the learning of words.

When they read orally, students encounter and express words in more than one sensory mode. They see, pronounce, and hear the words in the process, creating a representation of words with their own movements. The inclusion of multiple sensory modalities during oral reading makes the words more memorable, more deeply etched into memory, than through silent reading.

To help students hear their oral reading more clearly, many teachers I know use "whisper phones," often made of PVC pipe from a local hardware store. Students hold one end of the phone to their mouths and the other end to their ears while reading, which allows them to gauge their performance more easily.

Research on audio self-amplification, which is what whisper phones are designed to do, has demonstrated the potential these devices have in improving oral reading fluency, word decoding, and comprehension (Rasinski, 2002; Rasinski, Flexer, & Boomgarden-Szypulski, 2006). These devices not only have a positive effect on students' reading but also mask potential distractions such as talking and other sounds in the environment. Many of the students in these studies mentioned that hearing their voices clearly and distinctly while reading had a positive impact on their reading development.

Teacher-made "whisper phones" magnify students' auditory input while reading and mask extraneous noises.

Oral Reading Fosters Fluency

Like oral reading, reading fluency has, for years, been called the missing ingredient in many reading programs (Allington, 1983; Rasinski & Zutell, 1996). Perhaps this is because reading fluency was so closely tied to oral reading. However, all this changed with the report of the National Reading Panel (2000) confirming that fluency is important to reading success and must be a key component of effective instruction.

I have been a fluency advocate for over 30 years. It all began when, as a reading intervention teacher and graduate student in reading education in the late 1970s and early '80s, I found myself working with some elementary students that I had trouble figuring out. These were clearly bright students who seemed able to decode words they encountered in their reading and who understood the words they read. When I read to them, they had a solid understanding of those passages. Yet, despite their intelligence, despite their strengths in word decoding and vocabulary, despite their ability to comprehend texts read to them, when they were asked to read on their own, their comprehension faltered. How could it be that such bright students were experiencing difficulty in reading?

In my graduate studies, my professional reading had led me to some studies and papers that were beginning to revisit the concept of fluency as it applied to the reading program. Papers by Jay Samuels (1979), Carol Chomsky (1976), Richard Allington (1983), Peter Schreiber (1980), R. G. Heckelman (1969), Paul Hollingsworth (1978), and other literacy and language scholars were showing me that there was a critical and often ignored link between reading words and comprehension—that link was reading fluency. What I discovered through my reading and my work with children who were experiencing difficulty in learning to read was that although fluency may not be the answer to every student's problems in reading, reading comprehension, and overall reading achievement, it is the answer, or at least part of the answer, to many reading problems. I have become convinced that for reading instruction at all levels to be most effective, reading fluency must be a substantial and integral part of the curriculum.

Defining Fluency

Reading fluency refers to the ability of readers to read the words in text effortlessly and efficiently (automaticity) with meaningful expression that enhances the meaning of the text (prosody). Fluency takes phonics or word recognition to the next level. While many readers can decode words accurately, they may not be fluent or automatic in their word recognition. These readers tend to expend too much of their limited mental energy on figuring out the pronunciation and meaning of words, energy that is taken away from that more important task in reading comprehension—getting to the text's overall meaning. Thus, the lack of fluency often results in poor comprehension.

Fluent readers, on the other hand, are able to read words accurately and *effortlessly*. They recognize words and phrases instantly on sight. A minimal amount of cognitive energy is expended in decoding the words. This means, then, that the maximum amount of a reader's cognitive energy can be directed to the all-important task of making sense of the text. You are the best example of automaticity in word recognition as you read this book. I suspect that as a fluent reader you are having little trouble automatically recognizing the words I have written. Your instant recognition allows you to construct meaning as you move through the text.

There is also, however, a second component to fluency, one that is often forgotten by some programs for teaching fluency. That is prosody, or reading with expression. A key characteristic of fluent oral reading (or speech, for that matter) is the ability to embed appropriate expression into the reading.

Fluent readers raise and lower the volume and pitch of their voices, they speed up and slow down at appropriate places in the text, they read words in meaningful groups or phrases, they pause at appropriate places within the text. All these are elements of expression, or what linguists have termed prosody. Prosody is essentially the melody of language as it is read or spoken. By embedding prosody in our oral language (read or spoken), we are adding meaning to the text.

Brain researcher James Zull (2002) calls prosody "the other side of language." Zull argues that language comprehension generally occurs in the left hemisphere of the brain. "But there is another language function . . . in the other hemisphere, which may be equally important. This area understands the meaning of language that comes through emphasis on particular syllables—the rhythm, the pitch, the tone, and the inflection. These aspects of language together are called prosody, and they are of immense importance for meaning" (p. 171). Thus, even brain science is providing evidence that to work on prosody (an element of fluency) means to work on meaning (comprehension). Zull adds that approaches to integrating the cognitive aspects of language with prosody include reading aloud and having others read to us.

To be able to read with appropriate expression requires a reader to attend to meaning as he or she reads the text. So, when we work with a student on reading with expression (even when reading silently we tend to hear ourselves read), we are at the same time drawing that student's attention to meaning.

Fluency has often been called the bridge from phonics to comprehension. The link to phonics occurs when readers develop automaticity in their word recognition. The link to comprehension occurs when readers embed meaningful expression in their reading.

I often think of fluency as the gateway to comprehension. It may not be comprehension itself, but readers have to have some degree of fluency to comprehend what they read. In a review of reading comprehension strategies, cognitive psychologist Daniel Willingham (2007) concludes that comprehension strategies facilitate readers' understanding of texts and should be taught. However, he also notes that "students must have achieved some level of fluency for reading strategies to be effective." (p. 45).

Willingham is essentially describing the students who baffled me many years ago. They had no trouble comprehending text read to them. They had plenty of trouble comprehending text they had to read on their own. A major source of their comprehension problems was a lack of fluency. When these students read to me, they were slow, laborious, word-by-word, and expressionless in their reading. Moreover, they demonstrated little enthusiasm or understanding for what they read. Reading scholars Nell Duke, Michael Pressley, and Katherine Hilden (2004) suggest that a substantial number of students who struggle in reading comprehension have difficulties in fluency that are the source of their comprehension problems.

4 Ways to Build Reading Fluency

1. Model Good Oral Reading

Instruction in oral reading helps to develop fluency in several ways. First, when you read to your students orally, in a natural manner, you model fluent reading. Particularly when you draw attention to how you're reading, you help students see that meaning in reading is carried not only in the words, but also in the way the words are expressed. For example, you might contrast a fluent rendition of a passage with a more disfluent, labored, and word-by-word reading of it, then ask students which reading they preferred and why. Without a doubt, students will pick the more fluent reading. This becomes an important lesson in how they should read orally when given the opportunity.

Instruction that focuses too heavily on word-perfect decoding sends a message that good reading is nothing more than accurate word recognition. As a result, students tend to shoot for accuracy at the expense of everything else, including meaning. When asked to describe a good reader, struggling readers in our clinic often say that it is someone who reads all the words without making mistakes. Encouraging students to read accurately without paying attention to phrasing, expression, pacing, and, above all, comprehension may result in students reading like automatons: accurately, but without the sense of expression and understanding that is inherent in quality reading. Students who read only for accuracy often find themselves in the low reading groups, where they must listen to other students who read in a similar, disfluent fashion. Before these students can move up, they need to develop an internal understanding of what expressive, meaningful reading is all about. Modeling oral reading in a fluent manner is one way to make that happen.

2. Provide Oral Support or Assistance for Readers

Another way to develop fluency is through oral support of a student's own reading. When a student reads and hears simultaneously a fluent rendition of a text, as in a group or paired reading activity, his or her reading fluency and comprehension improve (Topping, 1987a, 1987b, 1995). There are many forms of supported reading, including choral reading, paired reading, and using recorded materials.

Choral Reading Choral reading happens often in the primary grades, but fades away in the intermediate and middle grades. This is unfortunate because choral reading builds fluency, as well as a sense of community, as mentioned earlier. The daily reading of a school motto, song, or other communal text unites students under a common sense of purpose.

Even the poorest, most disfluent student can benefit from choral reading. During choral reading, the student reads or attempts to read a text while at the same time hearing a more fluent reading of the same text by classmates and the teacher. When this is done on a regular and repeated basis, the student begins to internalize the fluent reading of the text being read, as well as other texts he or she may encounter. (For more information on choral reading, see Chapter 3.)

Paired Reading Paired reading is a form of assisted reading that involves two readers at opposite ends of the fluency spectrum. Keith Topping (1987a, 1989) first devised paired reading for parents who wanted to tutor their children, but he found that the substantive and positive effects of paired reading worked for other kinds of partnerships, including teacher-student and student-student.

The procedure for paired reading is quite simple. The more able reader (the tutor) and the less able reader sit side by side with a text chosen by the less able reader. The text may be a school assignment or a book that the student wishes to read for pleasure. The pair reads the text aloud together for 10 to 20 minutes. During the reading, the tutor adjusts his or her voice to match the reading fluency of the student. Whenever the student errs on a word, the tutor gives the correct pronunciation quickly and the reading continues to avoid disrupting fluency. The tutor also permits the less able student to maintain control over the reading experience; that student can opt to read on his or her own without the support of the tutor. Usually this is done with a nonverbal signal such as a gentle elbow in the tutor's ribs. The tutor remains quiet while the student reads on his or her own. Whenever the student falters, however, the tutor jumps in to support the student's reading.

Topping found that paired reading between struggling readers and their parents was very effective in improving general reading performance. He reported that parents engaging in paired reading with their children for approximately 15 minutes per day accelerated their child's reading growth by a factor of 3 to 5. That is, students who previously were making a half month's progress in reading for a month's worth of instruction would now, with the addition of paired reading, be making 1.5 to 2.5 months progress for every month of instruction. (For more information on paired reading, see Chapter 3.)

Since Topping's research was conducted, other forms of paired reading have emerged. Paired reading can take place between student and teacher, student and teacher aide or parent volunteer, and even student and student. The key is to have the child read orally with another, more fluent reader who provides support or assistance and adjusts the pace and volume to provide maximum assistance.

Using Recorded Materials If you are unable to support a child's reading through choral or paired reading, other options are available, such as using recorded materials or talking texts (Carbo, 1978a, 1981; Chomsky, 1976). The reader reads a text while simultaneously listening to a recorded fluent oral rendering of the same passage. As in other forms of assisted reading, students benefit by reading the text while simultaneously listening to the fluent oral rendition. A potential problem with talking texts, however, is lack of supervision. If another person does not sit next to the child, ensuring that he or she follows the printed text, the student may choose to listen to the story without reading it. When that happens, there is little improvement in reading. Nevertheless, reports of research on using recorded materials with struggling readers (Carbo, 1978a, 1978b; Chomsky, 1976) and English language learners (Koskinen et al., 1999, 2000) are impressive.

John Smith and Warwick Elley (1997) report on a study in New Zealand in which students listened to a book on tape while reading a print version of the same text. Students read and listened to the text repeatedly until they felt they could read it on their own, without the assistance of the recording. At that point, they moved on to another passage. These daily sessions lasted 20 to 30 minutes for 27 weeks, about three quarters of a school year. If we expect one month of gain for one month of instruction, the gains from the intervention were spectacular: nearly three times the expectations, or 2.2 years.

Pat Koskinen and her colleagues (Koskinen et al., 1999, 2000; Neumann & Koskinen, 1992) discovered that recorded texts have exceptional potential for improving the reading of English language learners. By giving ELL students texts and accompanying audiotapes to take home for practice, the researchers saw an increase in reading achievement, interest, and self-confidence in the students. The motivating effect of the tapes appeared to have a particularly powerful effect on the lowest-achieving students, who reported practicing reading more often at home than their higher-achieving peers.

Other research has pointed to the use of captioned television for improving fluency (Koskinen, Wilson, Gamrell, & Neuman, 1993; Koskinen, Bowen, Gambrell, Jensema, & Kane, 1997; Postlethwaite & Ross, 1992). While watching captioned television, readers simultaneously absorb both the spoken word and the printed text that flows across the screen. Thus, while reading the text, they are assisted by the oral rendition of the same text. (For more information on using recorded materials, see Chapter 3.)

3. Offer Plenty of Practice Opportunities—Wide and Deep, Oral and Silent

Whether you're learning to drive a car, bake a cake, make a jump shot in basketball, play a composition on the piano, knit a blanket, or type on a keyboard (as I am doing right now), practice is required to gain proficiency. The same is true for fluency.

When learning to drive a car, for instance, do you remember how awkward you felt the first time you sat behind the wheel? It required all your attention to coordinate the steering wheel, gearshift, ignition switch, floor pedals, and the other gadgets. Indeed, if the person in the passenger seat interrupted you, you probably found it annoying because it interfered with your concentration. However, after some practice, much of which involved driving down the same streets and making the same turns again and again, you developed a degree of fluency that enabled you to not only get around your neighborhood but anyplace where driving was permitted. Moreover, if you continued to drive, you are probably so fluent at it that you can now do other things while you drive—listen to the radio, converse with a passenger, or, as I have seen, put on makeup or shave while on the highway!

Practice is essential for reading fluency, too. When first learning to read, most students focus their attention on decoding the words that they confront. However, with practice, readers achieve fluency and can direct their attention toward making sense of the reading and away from the mechanics of decoding. This is true not only of passages that the readers have practiced but also of passages that they have never read before.

Generally, when we think of practice in reading, we think of wide reading, the kind of reading that most of us do as adults. Usually, when we finish reading a book, we move on to the next book. That is wide reading. Wide reading is also the form of practice that is embedded in most core reading programs. Once students have read a story in a core reading program and have engaged in discussion and some response activity with that story, they move on to the next story. Clearly, wide reading is a critical part of any reading program.

However, I would like to suggest another type of practice—deep practice. Sometimes our younger or struggling readers read a passage once, and they clearly do not read it well. If students read a passage poorly on the first attempt, and then we move them to the next passage, we are not allowing students to develop mastery or power over that or any other passage. Essentially, we are allowing students to practice mediocrity in their reading. Mediocre practice yields mediocre reading. Rather than moving on to the next passage to read, we need to give students an opportunity to reread this original passage more than once until they can read it with some degree of fluency and meaning. I call this deep reading, or rehearsal or repeated reading.

Repeated Readings Jay Samuels (1979) and others (Dowhower, 1994; Hasbrouck, Ihnot, & Rogers, 1999; National Reading Panel, 2000; Rasinski, et al, in press; Strecker, Roser, & Martinez, 1998; Therrien, 2004; Vaughn, Chard, Bryant, Coleman, & Kouzekanani, 2000) have documented that this particular form of practice, repeated reading, can lead to significant increases in students' fluency. Repeated reading can be done silently or orally, although oral repeated reading is the predominant and preferred form for developing fluency (National Reading Panel, 2000). Oral repeated readings provide additional sensory reinforcement for the reader, allowing him or her to focus on the prosodic (i.e., expressive) elements of reading that are essential to phrasing. Oral readings also ensure that the student is actually reading, not skimming or scanning, the text.

4. Encourage Fluency Through Phrasing

Besides being able to decode automatically, fluent readers chunk or parse text into syntactically appropriate units—mainly phrases (Rasinski, 1990). This is important because often meaning lies in a text's phrases and not in its individual words. The ability to separate a text into phrases aids comprehension. One of the most common characteristics of a disfluent reader is word-by-word reading. When a reader reads in this way, "chunking" a text appropriately becomes more difficult and, therefore, finding meaning in that text becomes more difficult as well. Consider the following sentence: *The young man the jungle gym.*

On first reading, the sentence may not make sense. And decoding, or understanding the meaning of any individual word, is most likely not what's causing difficulty. Your difficulty lies in phrasing. Most readers chunk the first portion of the sentence, "The young man . . .," into a phrase. But by doing that, they are left without a verb. Good readers generally go back and "rechunk" the text in a different manner, perhaps this way:

The young / man the jungle gym (i.e., *young* as a noun meaning a group of young people, and *man* as a verb meaning occupy).

While that sentence may seem a bit contrived, it illustrates nicely that good decoding and understanding of the words does not guarantee good comprehension and fluent reading. Fluent readers are able to decode well and chunk a text in ways that make its meaning more accessible.

In oral speech, phrasing is usually conveyed through prosodic cues (i.e., intonation, inflection, pauses, and so forth) in oral language. Say the following sentence to yourself aloud in a way that means the principal, not the teacher, is "the best in the school district":

The principal said the teacher is the best in the school district.

Notice how the inflections and intonations in your voice helped mark how the text should be phrased. You probably stressed the word *principal*, and your voice's pitch lowered at the phrase *said the teacher*.

Now try the same sentence in a way that declares the teacher as *the best* by the principal. Notice how your intonation changed to convey the different meaning. You most likely put greater stress on *teacher* and increased your pitch at *said the teacher*.

While phrasing in oral speech is marked by the speaker's intonation, in silent reading it tends to be marked by punctuation. (In the example above, the phrase *said the teacher* should have been enclosed in commas.) However, punctuation is not a foolproof marker of phrase boundaries. There are many cases in which written phrases are not marked by punctuation at all, such as in the first example: "The young man the jungle gym"—appropriate phrasing is important for comprehension, but there is no internal punctuation to mark the phrase boundaries.

Linguist Peter Schreiber (1980, 1987, 1991; Schreiber & Read, 1980) argues that reading fluency involves learning to chunk or parse written text into syntactically appropriate units or phrases. Since written punctuation is not totally reliable, the reader needs to infer phrase boundaries through his or her knowledge of oral speech patterns (prosody) and then apply that knowledge—usually, at first, through oral reading. As the reader orally reads a text several times, he or she begins to embed the expressive or prosodic patterns that mark phrase boundaries. This is not possible in an initial reading by someone who is not a fluent reader and who tends to read in a word-by-word fashion. Through oral reading, and especially oral repeated reading, the reader begins to bridge phrasing in oral speech and appropriate phrasing in reading written text. This knowledge of phrase patterns transfers to other, unfamiliar passages. Repeated oral reading, then, leads to fluency not just in decoding but also in meaningful phrasing. And improvements in fluency through word recognition and prosodic phrasing leads to improvements in reading in general, and better comprehension in particular.

Oral Reading Boosts Comprehension in Oral and Silent Reading

Oral reading can, indeed, foster comprehension. For example, a classic study found that by listening to their teacher read aloud to them over the course of a school year, students achieved better vocabulary and comprehension skills than students who had not been read to regularly by the teacher (Cohen, 1968). The positive effects of read aloud were significant even among the lowest-achieving students.

Moreover, when students read fluently, they use fewer of their limited attentional (or cognitive) resources for decoding and text chunking, and so can devote more attention to the more important part of reading: comprehension (LaBerge & Samuels, 1974). When they can apply more attention to comprehension, students obviously will understand better what they read. Finally, by focusing on oral reading fluency, students see that words are not the only part of the text that carry meaning. Meaning is also carried through the intonation, expression, phrasing, and pausing that are essential to fluent reading.

A 1995 study (Pinnell, Pikulski, Wixson, Campbell, Gough, & Beatty) and a 2005 replication (Daane, Campbell, Grigg, Goodman, & Oranje) sponsored by the United States Department of Education demonstrated the strong association between oral reading fluency and silent reading comprehension. In the original study, over a thousand fourth graders were asked to read a passage aloud. Their oral rendition was rated on a four-point rubric (see Chapter 8) by trained raters; a score of 4 reflected fluent and expressive oral reading, while a score of 1 reflected a disfluent, word-by-word reading. The same fourth graders were then given a test that measured their comprehension of a set of passages that they read silently. The fourth graders who were the most fluent readers were also the best comprehenders. Moreover, every decline in oral reading fluency was marked by a corresponding decline in silent reading comprehension. The students who read best orally also scored highest in silent reading comprehension. And those students who struggled most with oral reading, even though they read with a high level of accuracy, also had the most difficulty in reading comprehension. The replication study ten years later with close to 1,500 students found much the same results. In addition, in both studies, a significant number (close to half) of all students were not sufficiently fluent in reading and were also manifesting significant difficulties in comprehension.

The children in our reading clinic at Kent State University often come with school reports noting that comprehension is their major problem. A closer examination of their reading usually confirms that comprehension is indeed a problem, along with difficulty in reading fluency. In fact, the students' lack of fluency, in most cases, is at least one cause of their comprehension problem. The students struggle so much with fluency, and in putting so much cognitive effort into the task of making it through a passage, that little is left over for understanding the text. For these students, we often focus our initial efforts on building their oral reading fluency abilities (what I will share with you in Chapters 2–7).

In the majority of cases, this work in fluency leads to significant gains in comprehension. Once a student's attention is freed up to deal with comprehension, comprehension improves.

Oral Reading Allows Us to View the Reading Process

Reading may not be a solitary act. It is, however, an internal act. Much of what happens during reading happens in the head. Unless we use brain mapping or scanning methodologies, we have a difficult time seeing what actually happens inside a reader's head during reading.

Oral reading provides the next best thing. We can, for example, assess a reader's word decoding by determining the percentage of words decoded correctly in a passage that the student reads orally. A student should be able to decode text written at her or his grade level with an accuracy rate in the range of 92 to 98 percent (Rasinski & Padak, 2005a, 2005b). Accuracy rates significantly below that target rate may be a sign of serious difficulty in decoding.

Reading specialists can analyze students' oral reading errors to diagnose reading problems. Do decoding errors tend to fall in the beginning, middle, or end of words? Does the student tend to err on one-syllable words or words of greater length? Do the decoding errors make sense within the overall meaning of the sentence or passage? Are the errors syntactically or grammatically acceptable within the passage? Does the error give evidence that the reader is applying phonics and other word-decoding skills? Is the reader aware of making errors and able to explain his or her thinking in making those errors? Answers to these questions can give a trained reading specialist helpful data that will identify relative strengths and weaknesses and inform your instruction.

The automaticity component of reading fluency can also be assessed by determining the reader's reading rate (usually calculated by the number of words read correctly per minute on grade-level text). A reader who is fluent (automatic) in his or her decoding skills will be able to read at a fairly rapid pace and with expression. We have fairly good norms for students' ability to read various grade-level materials at different times of the year. Significant deviations from these norms can provide clues about each student's development in reading fluency. Moreover, by listening to children read and rating their performance on a descriptive rubric scale for prosody, we can get an overall sense of their fluency and ability to make sense of the passage. In my own dissertation study as well as a follow-up study (Rasinski, Rikli, & Johnston, 2009), I found that quick ratings of third-, fifth-, and eighth-grade students' oral reading turned out to be a strong and significant way to predict their overall reading proficiency on a standardized silent-reading comprehension test. (For more information on assessing oral reading, see Chapter 8.)

➤ Concluding Thoughts

Oral reading plays a significant role in effective reading instruction. It is an important tool in any teacher's kit of instructional strategies. In the earliest grades, oral reading may take on a primary role in instruction. Over time, however, that role gives way to silent reading. Indeed, by the intermediate and middle grades, oral reading generally plays more of a supporting role in reading instruction. However, to say that oral reading plays a supporting role in the middle grades does not mean that it should have no role at all. At any grade level through adulthood, there are many occasions for which oral reading is not only appropriate, but also preferred and necessary.

Oral reading can make reading instruction more varied, more interesting, and more effective. School administrator Davis Eidhal from Ottumwa, Iowa, wrote to me, after the publication of the first edition of this book, that employing methods of oral reading fluency in his schools led to improvements in students' overall reading performance in the elementary and middle grades. The improvements were particularly striking for the struggling readers.

The key is knowing how to use oral reading to its full potential to improve word recognition, reading fluency, and comprehension. In the following chapters, I'll show you how.

Chapter 2

Read Aloud

Modeling Fluent Reading and Motivating Readers

"I learned from the age of two or three that any room in our house, at any time of the day, was there to read in, or be read to. My mother read to me. . . . She was an expressive reader. When she was reading 'Puss in Boots,' for instance, it was impossible not to know that she distrusted all cats. . . . Ever since I was first read to, then started reading to myself, there has never been a line read that I didn't hear."

—Eudora Welty

Many of us have vivid childhood memories of being read to by a parent, grandparent, or teacher. There was something special about listening to an enjoyable story in the comforting company of a trusted adult. It probably comes as no surprise, then, that one of my favorite classroom activities is reading to students or watching teachers read to their students. At the schools I visit, just before read aloud, there is often a lot of nervous energy among the students as they take their seats or sit on the floor in front of the teacher. But their squirming, giggling, and chatting quickly dissipate as the teacher begins to read and transports the class to another place and time. The look of enchantment on children's faces during read aloud says it all. Students not only love stories, but they also love having stories read to them.

There is something very special about reading aloud—no matter who is doing the oral reading. Writer Verlyn Klinkenborg (2009), whom I quoted at the beginning of Chapter 1, says that "reading aloud recaptures the physicality of words. To read with your lungs and diaphragm, with your tongue and lips, is very different than reading with your eyes alone. The language becomes a part of the body." Reading aloud is a good way to "learn something important about the rhythms of language . . . it reveals how far into the words—and the pattern of the words—the reader really sees" (p. 2). I would argue that by listening to material read aloud, the listener experiences much of what Klinkenborg is talking about.

As much as read aloud is an affective, aesthetic, and emotional experience, it is a powerful learning experience as well. Certainly, children in read alouds learn about the content of the material being read, but read aloud also helps them in learning to read. In her seminal study of children who learned to read before starting formal schooling, Dolores Durkin (1966) found that regular oral reading to children by parents was one of the key factors in children's early success.

➤ The Benefits of Read Aloud

Clearly, read aloud builds interest in reading, but its benefits do not end there. Read aloud also helps you achieve three important goals with your students: it improves comprehension and vocabulary, increases fluency, and builds motivation.

Improves Comprehension and Vocabulary

Read aloud exposes students to texts that they may not find on their own or may not be able to read on their own. And when students are exposed to these different and/or more sophisticated texts through read aloud, their vocabulary and comprehension improve (Cohen, 1968).

Cunningham and Stanovich (1998) argue that the act of reading or being read to develops the mind and increases intelligence. Citing work by other scholars, they note that most printed material, even a children's book, has more sophisticated words than nearly any other form of oral language. For example, they note that the level of vocabulary in storybooks for preschoolers is at approximately the same level as speech between college graduates. Cunningham and Stanovich also note that written language is qualitatively different from oral language, and that, through reading and being read to, readers and listeners are exposed to vocabulary that they would not likely encounter in oral language. Words such as *infinite, exposure, literal, luxury, maneuver, provoke,* and *relinquish* are much more likely to be found in written text than in oral speech. Through being read to, students can handle material that they may not be able to handle on their own and thus may be exposed to more sophisticated vocabulary. When students are asked to listen for interesting words during read aloud that are then posted on a chart afterward (Blachowicz & Fisher, 2009), they become even more aware of the wonderful words that authors use in their writing, and they're more likely to want to use such words in their own writing experiences.

Beck and McKeown (2001) note that read aloud provides rich opportunities for students to develop their understanding of decontextualized language, language that is more likely to be found in written text and not in oral speech. Reading aloud is also key to developing students' comprehension skills, especially when the experience contains opportunities to engage in discussions about the text or what Beck and McKeown call "text talk." Discussions can be used to encourage listeners to construct more than literal meaning, connect ideas within and beyond the text, use their background knowledge, and ponder sophisticated words from the text. This all builds comprehension skills by giving readers a platform to construct deep and critical understandings of texts.

Increases Fluency

During read aloud, the listener hears how the reader's voice can be used to create and extend meaning. Through intonation, expression, phrasing, and pausing at appropriate points, the reader demonstrates that meaning is embedded in more than just the words; it's also in the interpretation of the words. By reading orally to students, we model what fluent, meaningful reading is like (Rasinski & Padak, 2008). We send a message to students that whether they read both orally and silently, they need to read in the same expressive, meaningful manner.

Builds Motivation

Perhaps more than anything else, being read to is a purely enjoyable experience. It nurtures a desire in students to read on their own. Jim Trelease (2006) perhaps says it best in his book *The Read-Aloud Handbook*: "Every time we read to a child, we're sending a 'pleasure' message to the child's brain. You could even call it a commercial, conditioning the child to associate books and print with pleasure" (p. 5).

Although we often associate read aloud with preschool and elementary grades, and know that the frequency of read-aloud experiences declines as students move up the grades (Hoffman, Roser, & Battle, 1993), students of all ages love to be read to. In a study of the factors that motivate middle-grade students to read, for example, Ivey and Broaddus (2001) found that being read to by the teacher was second only to free reading as the activity students enjoyed most. Over 60 percent of the students identified teacher read aloud as a preferred activity. Further, Charlotte Huck (1977) notes that a well-planned read-aloud program, even for older students, can stimulate interest in books and introduce them to quality literature in various genres, well beyond their reading level. Even as an adult, I love to hear books read to me. When my wife and I travel by car, we always begin by stopping at our local library to check out some audio books. And, while on the road, we seem to stop at every Cracker Barrel restaurant we pass to rent a new book to listen to on our car's CD player!

For these reasons—the development of vocabulary, comprehension, fluency, and a motivation to read—daily oral reading should happen at every grade level, at least through middle school. (For more information on the benefits of read aloud, see Chapter 1, pages 25–26.)

➤ Preparing for Read Aloud

There is no secret to reading aloud to children in a classroom. You just have to do it. However, the following considerations may help you make the most of the experience.

Timing

Choose a time for read aloud that is relaxed, quiet, and conducive to listening. For many teachers in self-contained classrooms, after lunch is best. For other teachers, the ideal time might be first thing in the morning, right before lunch, or at the very end of the day. For some lucky students, there may be even more than one read-aloud period per day.

How long should you read? The answer will vary depending on your personal style and preference, as well as the nature of your schedule and group. Generally, 10 to 30 minutes is appropriate.

Atmosphere

Setting the mood for read aloud is important, too. Lower the lights in the room, especially the overhead lights. Have a desk or table lamp available for you to read by and a special chair to read from. Some teachers use a bar stool so they can see the entire group and project their voices. Others prefer a rocking chair to give the experience a warm, homey feel. Invite students to sit in front of you on a carpet. This arrangement works well not only for primary students, but for upper elementary and middle school students as well.

Book Selection

What are the best books to read to students? The answer is different for everyone, but I offer criteria for choosing wisely on the next page. Whatever you choose, keep in mind one of the main purposes of read aloud: to develop in students a love of reading and books.

Consider Your Favorites

Read aloud the books you like to students. Your enthusiasm will come through. Keep a log of all the books you enjoy and would like to share with students. When you come across a new book, ask yourself if it would be a good candidate for read aloud. In *The Read-Aloud Handbook*, Jim Trelease provides readers with his own list of more than 300 favorites, based on his extensive experience working with children of all ages.

Reach Beyond Students' Comfort Zone

Think of books that students may not pick up on their own because the text is difficult or unfamiliar. By reading such books to students, you expose them to more sophisticated words, sentences, content, and ideas, which builds their vocabulary and comprehension skills. Be sure to include the very best books in various genres. Most students in elementary and middle grades like to read contemporary fiction with characters who remind them of themselves. Use a read aloud to expose students to historical fiction, biography, science fiction and fantasy, poetry, and folktales.

Make Connections

Try to find books that connect to life in your classroom and to other texts students may be reading or experiencing (Hartman & Hartman, 1993). For example, books that complement a forthcoming unit of study will help build students' background knowledge and interest. Find books that connect to the season, holidays, or special events. These kinds of choices will strengthen and extend students' awareness of a topic (Rasinski & Padak, 2000).

Focus on Award Winners

If your knowledge of books is limited, rely on the expertise of others by focusing on books that have won awards, in particular the Newbery and Caldecott awards. The Newbery Medal is given yearly by the American Library Association to the "most distinguished contribution to American literature for children." Each year, one book is selected as the Newbery winner and several others are named Honor

Books. Similarly, the Caldecott Medal is given yearly to the "most distinguished American picture book for children." As with the Newbery, there is one winner and usually several Honor Books. (See Figure 2.1 on page 52 for sources to help you find medal winners and honor books.)

Read Professional Journals

The International Reading Association (IRA) offers teachers several wonderful resources for finding books that students like to read or hear. Perhaps the best known is Children's Choices, a yearly compilation of new books that have been read by approximately 10,000 elementary and middle-grade students throughout the United States. The students vote on their favorites, and the finalists are identified as Children's Choice books. Usually more than a hundred books are identified and described.

Children's Choices are published annually in the October issue of *The Reading Teacher*, IRA's professional journal for preschool, elementary, and middle-grade teachers. (See Figure 2.1 on page 52 for more information on Children's Choices.) In its November issue, *The Reading Teacher* features an annual list of approximately 30 titles that teachers feel are among the very best of recent vintage for children. Finally, you'll find a thematic review of recently published children's books in every issue.

IRA also publishes the *Journal of Adolescent and Adult Literacy (JAAL)*, which is for teachers of middle and secondary grades. Each year in its November issue, *JAAL* publishes Young Adults' Choices, a list of approximately 30 recent titles for adolescents and young adults that have been identified by students as their favorites. (See Figure 2.1 on page 52 for more information on Young Adults' Choices.)

Rely on Your Librarian, Colleagues, and the Internet

One of the very best resources for information on books is a human resource: the community or school librarian. These specialists are well aware of the kinds of books that can motivate and enchant listeners. Also, be sure to chat with booksellers at your local bookstores. And, of course, I think we have all found what a wonderful resource the Internet has become. A few well-defined searches on the Internet can yield many excellent titles. (Although the Internet is not itself a human resource, the information placed on it does originate with people.)

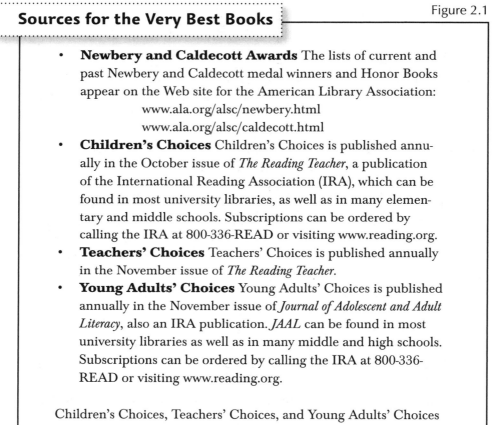

Figure 2.1

Sources for the Very Best Books

- **Newbery and Caldecott Awards** The lists of current and past Newbery and Caldecott medal winners and Honor Books appear on the Web site for the American Library Association:
  www.ala.org/alsc/newbery.html
  www.ala.org/alsc/caldecott.html
- **Children's Choices** Children's Choices is published annually in the October issue of *The Reading Teacher*, a publication of the International Reading Association (IRA), which can be found in most university libraries, as well as in many elementary and middle schools. Subscriptions can be ordered by calling the IRA at 800-336-READ or visiting www.reading.org.
- **Teachers' Choices** Teachers' Choices is published annually in the November issue of *The Reading Teacher*.
- **Young Adults' Choices** Young Adults' Choices is published annually in the November issue of *Journal of Adolescent and Adult Literacy*, also an IRA publication. *JAAL* can be found in most university libraries as well as in many middle and high schools. Subscriptions can be ordered by calling the IRA at 800-336-READ or visiting www.reading.org.

Children's Choices, Teachers' Choices, and Young Adults' Choices can also be accessed and downloaded at no cost from the IRA Web site: www.reading.org.

Keep an eye and ear open to other teachers as well. Usually, they have classroom-tested favorites for read aloud that they are happy to share. I have been in the reading business for more than 30 years and have read a lot of books for children. Still, after all this time, I am always discovering new books for read aloud. Usually, recommendations come from teachers in my courses who have found books to which students respond well.

Think Beyond Books

Essays, columns, reviews, and articles of interest from local and national newspapers and magazines are great for read aloud, too. Check the Internet for a huge variety of other materials that may be appropriate to share with students. By doing so, you show that print worth sharing and of value is available from a wide variety of sources.

Select for Voice

Look for materials that have a strong voice. Voice is that characteristic of writing where readers can hear the voice of the author (and characters) as they read the text orally or silently. Voice in writing is the flip side of prosody, or expression in reading. As I mentioned in Chapter 1, prosody is a key element of reading fluency. Materials that we read to students (and have students read on their own) that have a strong voice are naturals for helping them become aware of the importance of prosody in reading.

Practice, Practice, Practice

What makes read aloud special is hearing how the expressive voice of the reader adds meaning and energy to the reading of a text. That expressiveness comes from practice. Once you've chosen a text, read it over in advance once or twice. Familiarize yourself with the characters and the plot. Identify points at which to insert dramatic pauses, to raise and lower your voice, to increase your volume or to read in a whisper, to speed up or slow down, etc.

I often ask my undergraduate students to read to children whenever they visit a classroom. To many of them, it seems like an easy task, so they do little to prepare. However, once they get in front of a group of eager and enthusiastic children, they often become a bit anxious, which results in reading with a flat voice, poor phrasing, and many hesitations and errors. And, of course, the children aren't all that satisfied with the read aloud. The lesson for all of us, then, is to practice beforehand.

The primary purpose of read aloud is to provide students with an enjoyable literary experience. We often use read aloud to introduce students to unfamiliar genres or authors or to challenge them with texts they'd struggle with on their own. Experiences like these not only satisfy the listener, but they also provide a model of fluent, meaningful reading. In this sense, read aloud is a window into the reading process for students who are still developing. It is imperative, then, that we practice to provide them with the most fluent, and expressive, example possible.

See a read aloud in action on the DVD.

➤ Conducting Read Aloud

You've picked a time to read. You've chosen and practiced your reading. You've created a mood. Now it's time to read aloud. There are two important points to consider: (1) setting the stage to convey the importance of the experience, and (2) thinking aloud to help students view how a good reader approaches a text.

Setting the Stage

I often begin read aloud by lighting a ritual candle and reciting a familiar quote or poem to set the mood. This communicates that something special is about to happen. I particularly like to use the Shel Silverstein (1974) poem "Invitation." This simple poem, when read aloud, signals to students that we are about to do something very special—read!

Similarly, I often use a poem to bring the read aloud to an end. I like this one by Lee Bennett Hopkins (1990), "Good Books, Good Times!" which can be read by the teacher or by the class, chorally, or in groups.

> *Good books.*
> *Good times.*
> *Good stories.*
> *Good rhymes.*
> *Good beginnings.*
> *Good ends.*
> *Good people.*
> *Good friends.*
> *Good fiction.*
> *Good facts.*

Good adventures.
Good acts.
Good stories.
Good rhymes.
Good books.
Good times.

Beginning and ending each read-aloud session with a quote or poem communicates to students the importance and value of the event.

Thinking Aloud

Read aloud allows developing readers to view fluent and meaningful reading, but we can occasionally make the reading process even more transparent by thinking aloud. When you think aloud, you stop the reading from time to time and share how you're negotiating the text and constructing meaning. For example, you may make an error while reading aloud, on purpose or by accident. This provides a wonderful opportunity to show students what good readers do when they run into difficulty. When you make an error, stop reading and share your thinking. Here's an example:

Text: After the ballgame I went to the movies with my friends.

Teacher: "After the ballgame I went to the movies with my freds." Freds? Does that make sense?

Several students: No.

Teacher: Let me try that again. "After the ballgame I went to the movies with my . . ." Okay, who would I go to the movies with? Maybe Fred, but there is not a Fred in the story. No, it needs to be someone who has been mentioned before. Let me take a closer look at that word, f-r-i-e-n-d-s. Oh, that word is *friends*, of course. The story so far has been about what I do with my two best buddies, and another name for buddies is friends.

At other points in the text, you might stop and offer predictions about what will come next based on the events thus far and the background knowledge you possess. Here's an example from a teacher reading *Just a Dream* by Chris Van Allsburg (1990):

Teacher: Wow, that was quite a dream that Walter had. He had a glimpse into what the future might be like if people didn't take care of the environment. I wonder what will happen next? Hmmm. Since the story began by showing some of the ways Walter didn't care for the environment, I wonder if now he will do something about those things.

At other times you might debate with yourself over the meaning of certain lines or ideas in the text.

Thinking aloud can become tedious if you do too often. But when you use it strategically for particular purposes, thinking aloud helps students see that reading is more than a matter of reading the words as quickly and accurately as possible. It is thinking, problem solving, and meaning making. Later, after you've modeled the process, individual students can share their own think alouds with you and classmates (Oster, 2001).

Good readers—readers who understand what they read—often carry on a conversation with themselves during reading. Thinking aloud while reading aloud allows you to show students how this conversation might take place.

➤Responding After Read Aloud

No read-aloud experience is complete without giving students an opportunity to respond to what they have heard. Jean Piaget noted that learning requires two acts: assimilation, in which experience or information comes into the learner, and accommodation, in which the learner adjusts him- or herself to the learned experience or information (Piaget & Inhelder, 1969). Reading requires similar acts. The reader takes in information from the text. To fully understand that text, however, he or she must respond in some meaningful way to the reading experience.

As adults, we often find ourselves discussing a book or newspaper article with a spouse or friend, arguing with ourselves about a provocative passage, writing a letter to the editor in response to a magazine or newspaper article, finding out more information about something we've read. All of these actions are meaningful responses to our reading and help us take our understanding of what we have read to a deeper level.

In their survey of read-aloud experiences in elementary schools, Hoffman, Roser, and Battle (1993) found that most teachers engaged in discussion about the reading for five minutes before or after the read aloud. Moreover, the researchers found that other types of response activities, such as writing, drawing, and dramatizing, were offered to students in less than a quarter of the read-aloud experiences they observed.

Creative and varied ways to allow students to respond to read aloud should be a regular part of the experience. Below are some of the best activities I've discovered.

Oral Response

A brief follow-up discussion is an effective and easy way to allow students to respond to a read aloud. Discussions should be open-ended and challenge students to think deeply and critically about what they have heard (Beck & McKeown, 2001), so asking the right questions is essential. For example, after reading Peggy Rathmann's (1995) *Officer Buckle and Gloria*, you might ask the following questions:

- What did you like most about this story? Why?
- What did you like least? Why?
- Why did the family call Harry a "strange dog"?
- How would you describe the main character? Why?
- What do you think Gloria was thinking when she began doing her "tricks" during Officer Buckle's talks?
- What do you think will happen next in this story? How do you think Gloria will act during Officer Buckle's next school presentation? Why do you think so?
- Do you know anyone like Gloria? How is this person like Gloria? How is this person different from Gloria?
- If the author wrote another book about this character, what would you expect to happen?

If your primary goal is to develop vocabulary, you might ask students to think about their favorite word or expression from the read aloud. List those words and expressions on chart paper, ask students to explain the reasons for their choices, and challenge them to use the words and expressions in their own oral and written language. You might also ask students to sort the words into categories they select. Figure 2.2, for example, shows how a group of students sorted words chosen from Van Allsburg's *Just a Dream*.

Figure 2.2

Words That Make Beautiful Pictures	Words that Make Pictures That Are Not Beautiful
tree	trash
breeze	fire hydrant
rustling leaves	medicine
Everest	dull yellow haze
birthday present	bulldozer

How third graders sorted words from Just a Dream

If your goal is to develop a greater awareness of fluency, you would want to talk with your students about how you were able to make meaning with your voice as you read aloud. Ask students to talk about what they were thinking when you raised or lowered your voice, changed the pace of your reading, or inserted a dramatic pause. Teaching is a process of making visible what is often invisible for students. By making reading with expression a point of discussion, you are helping to make visible for students that element in reading that often occurs below their radar. Because expression in reading helps with comprehension, students are often not even aware of their teacher's expression.

When you begin reading to your students, sometimes try reading in an excessively fast or slow manner or in a monotone, without expression. You won't be able to read for long before your students will react negatively. At that point, ask them what was wrong with your reading—note that you read all the words correctly. Sometimes, we learn from a negative example, and students quickly discover that it is not the words alone that carry the meaning, but it is also how the words are phrased, emphasized, and read with the appropriate expression.

A follow-up discussion doesn't always have to happen right after reading. It can happen the following day. Before the next read aloud, simply ask students to summarize or respond to the previous day's reading and make predictions about what is to come.

It's important for all students to respond in a meaningful and personal way. If you have one large class discussion, some students may be left out. To avoid that, ask students to join partners or small groups, think about the read aloud for a few minutes, and then share their responses. (This is sometimes called Think, Pair, Share.) When several discussions are taking place simultaneously, you can be sure that each student has an opportunity to share his or her thoughts on the book.

Visual Response

Good stories evoke rich images in the mind. The National Reading Panel identified imagery as a good tool for developing and promoting comprehension in students. To use imagery, ask students to draw a favorite scene from a story. Then have them share and explain their drawings, and use the drawings as the basis for further discussion of the text. Usually, students will include items in their drawings that are not in the story. These added touches may be inferences or educated guesses, a form of higher-level thinking. To create them, students must use their background knowledge as well as the text information.

One of my favorite visual response activities is called Sketch-to-Stretch (Harste, Short, & Burke, 1988). In small groups, students draw a favorite scene from a story that has been read to them—a literal interpretation of events or something more abstract or thematic. Each student then shares his or her drawing with others in the group, who "stretch" to determine what is being portrayed. This activity often requires students to make inferences about the text and the drawing, in other words, to engage in higher-level thinking.

Induced imagery (Gambrell, Kapinus, & Wilson, 1987) is another powerful activity. Students talk about the images they made in their minds while listening to (or reading) a story. Try using induced imagery by following these steps.

1. Choose a passage from a book that is rich with description.
2. Read a line or two to students and share the pictures you see developing in your mind.
3. Ask students to share their own images and explain what caused them to form. Compare and contrast the students' various images. Notice the differences and similarities between images, even though they came from the same text.

4. At natural stopping points, ask students to refine their images. Model this by sharing and adjusting your own image, based on what you read.

5. Ask students to adjust and describe their own images, and then compare and contrast the various images again. Use the development of images as the focus of discussion for the story.

Written Response

It is always a good idea to ask students to write about what they have read or what has been read to them. You can have students make daily open-ended entries in journals, where they are free to write whatever they wish about the read aloud. Figure 2.3 on page 61 shows a fourth-grade student's open-ended response to teacher Kathy Perfect's reading of *Roll of Thunder, Hear My Cry* (Taylor, 1976). You can also give students writing prompts, including the following:

- Write about what will happen next in this story. (Asking students to make and justify predictions about upcoming events in a story is often called a Directed Reading-Thinking Activity [Stauffer, 1980] or a Directed Listening-Thinking Activity.)
- Describe the character as you see him or her in your mind.
- Why do you or do you not think the character is acting in a good, decent manner?
- Pretend that a character died at this point in the story. Write an obituary or epilogue for that person.
- Describe an event in your own life that reminds you of one in the story. Be sure to note similarities and differences.
- Write a letter to the main character giving him or her advice on how to handle his or her problem.
- What would have been a good title for this chapter in the story?

Figure 2.3

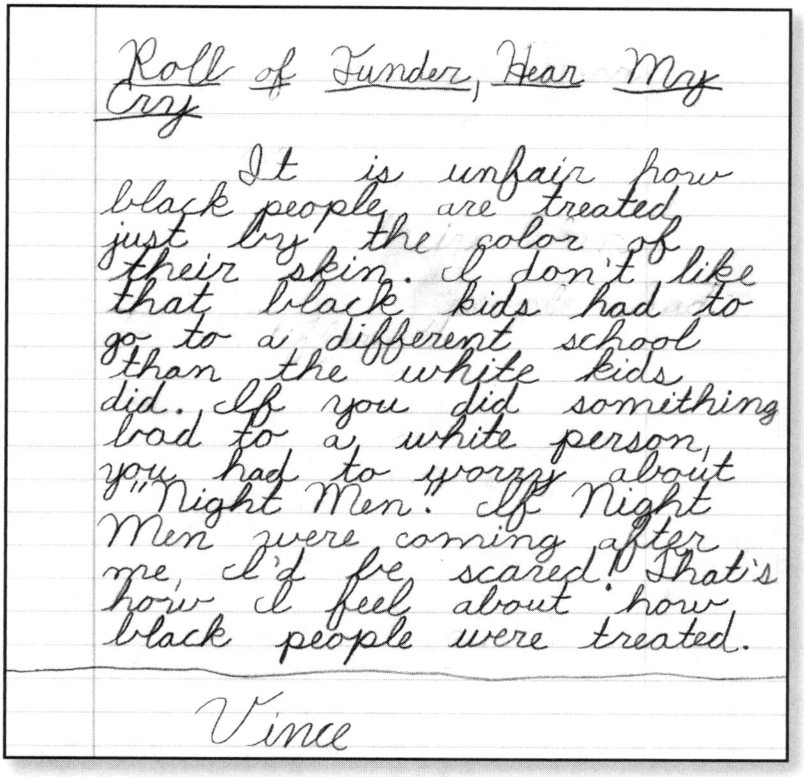

> # Roll of Junder, Hear My Cry
>
> It is unfair how black people, are treated just by the color of their skin. I don't like that black kids had to go to a different school than the white kids did. If you did something bad to a white person, you had to worry about "Night Men." If Night Men were coming after me, I'd be scared! That's how I feel about how black people were treated.
>
> Vince

Fourth-grader Vince's open-ended response to
Roll of Thunder, Hear My Cry

After reading a segment of *Roll of Thunder, Hear My Cry*, teacher Kathy Perfect asked her fourth graders to make a prediction about the next chapter in the book. Figure 2.4 on page 62 shows a student's response. Teacher Julie McClish prompted her second graders to write about their own very bad day after she read them *Alexander and the Terrible, Horrible, No Good, Very Bad Day* (Viorst, 1972). Figure 2.5 on page 63 shows predictions from two students.

Both open-ended and prompted responses should be offered to students on a regular and balanced basis. After writing, ask volunteers to share their responses with the whole class or in small groups.

Figure 2.4

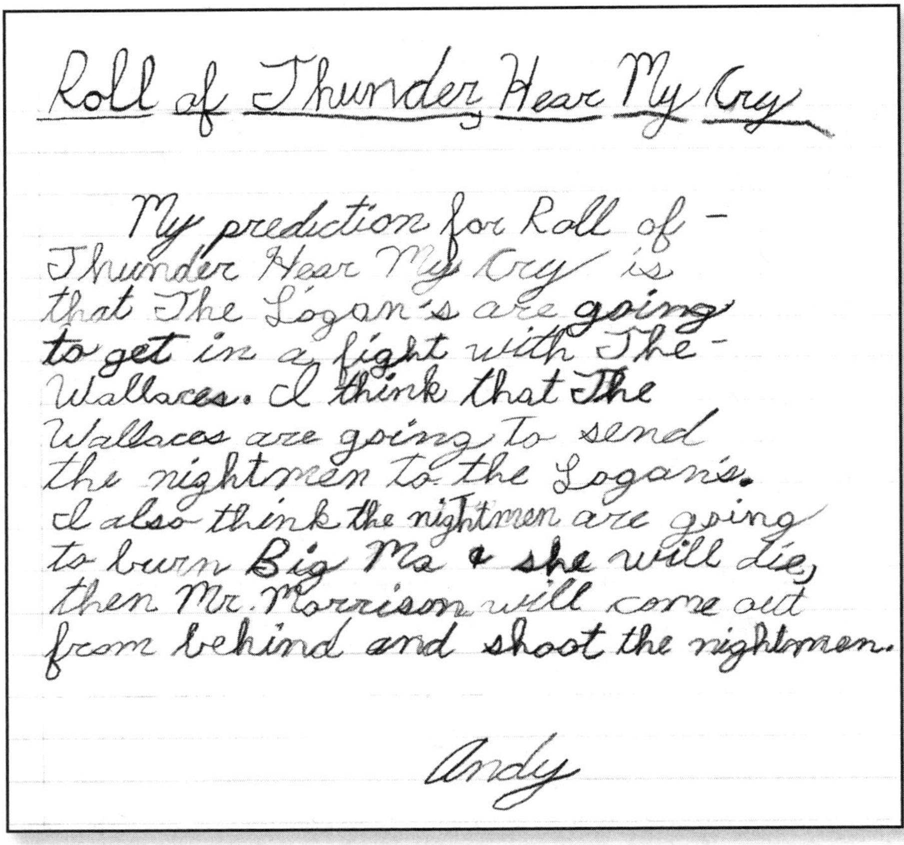

Roll of Thunder, Hear My Cry

My prediction for Roll of -
Thunder Hear My Cry is
that The Logan's are going
to get in a fight with The -
Wallaces. I think that The
Wallaces are going to send
the nightmen to the Logan's.
I also think the nightmen are going
to burn Big Ma & she will die,
then Mr. Morrison will come out
from behind and shoot the nightmen.

Andy

Andy's prediction for Roll of Thunder, Hear My Cry

Figure 2.5

After their teacher read
Alexander and the Terrible,
Horrible, No Good, Very Bad Day,
*Heather and Melissa wrote about
their own very bad days.*

I had a bad day
wene me barby
hed brock of.

The book made me think about a bad
day because when my sister Rude
to me. and when my sister would call
me a louser.

Physical Response

Some students find it easiest to represent meaning through movement. Using the body is a legitimate and creative way to encourage response and promote deep comprehension. One of the most effective forms of physical response is "tableau" (Wilhelm, 2002). Groups of students choose a significant event from a story and represent it as a "freeze frame picture," using their bodies as the elements in the picture. Students can also represent the event by turning their bodies into statues. Each student in the group must participate in the tableau, even if it means becoming a tree, a door, an animal, or some other non-human object.

Once students have chosen an event and planned how to represent it, they present their tableau to their classmates, getting into position when the teacher calls out "one, two, freeze." From there, the audience tries to guess what event the group is portraying. Students creating the tableau have reason to discuss the story before the performance as they plan, and students in the audience discuss the story during the performance as they attempt to identify the event.

After reading aloud Peggy Rathmann's *Officer Buckle and Gloria*, for example, a teacher divides her first-grade class into groups of four. Each group is asked to create a tableau based on a significant event in the story. The groups engage in animated discussions as they choose their events and plan their tableaux. Then, one group after another makes its presentation. Several groups depict Officer Buckle giving his safety lecture in school, with Gloria standing in the background, mocking him good-naturedly. Other groups create tableaux representing Officer Buckle's despair when he finds out about Gloria's antics. Still others portray Gloria's less-than-inspiring safety presentation after Officer Buckle chooses to stop giving the lectures himself.

If the audience cannot determine the event, the group gives more information. To do this, the teacher taps one or more members of the tableau group. That member breaks out of his or her "freeze" and either utters a line in character (even inanimate objects are allowed to talk) or makes a gesture that relates to the person or object being portrayed. This series of events continues until all the tableau groups have made their presentations.

As students become more adept at creating tableaux, the nature of the tableaux often changes—from literal portrayals of scenes to more abstract portrayals of themes, morals, or ideas. For example, when students who listened to *Officer Buckle and Gloria* were asked to summarize the story in tableau, they captured the essence of the story perfectly by portraying two pals standing together, arm in arm.

Tableaux have many applications beyond read aloud. Many teachers find them a challenging way for students to portray meaning in social studies, history, art, or other subject areas.

Tableaux are not only fun, they're also safe for all students. When given time to plan and practice tableaux, students who are not gifted physically or verbally can shine in the classroom. As their abilities and confidence grow, those students can move on to other forms of performance representation, such as mime, story theater (one or more students read the text while others perform the events of the story in pantomime style), puppetry, or expressive movement and dance.

➤ Concluding Thoughts

All reading experiences are more productive when students are given opportunities to respond in some way to the text. The read-aloud experience is no exception. However, because the text is shared, read aloud helps students build comprehension in two ways: (1) by responding to the text on a personal level, and (2) by exchanging responses with others.

In addition to building comprehension by listening to a teacher or another adult read to them, students discover the fluency dimension of reading—that meaning is shared not only by the words that are read, but also by the way in which those words are expressed. This is the essence of fluency.

Chapter 3

Assisted Reading

Providing a Scaffold for Your Developing and Struggling Readers

"My mother always sang to her children. Her voice came out just a little bit in the minor key. 'Wee Willie Winkie's' song was wonderfully sad when she sang the lullabies. 'Oh, but now there's a record. She could have her own record to listen to,' my father would have said. For there came a Victrola record of 'Bobby Shafftoe' and 'Rock-a-Bye Baby,' all of Mother's lullabies, which could be played to take her place. Soon I was able to play her my own lullabies all day long."

—Eudora Welty

In the previous chapter, I made the point that read aloud is a superb way to model oral reading. Indeed, we often learn by watching a more expert person do the task we are attempting to master. However, we not only learn by watching that person, but also by attempting the task alongside him or her. We learn by doing, especially when we are supported by someone who can guide us, show us how, and help us until we are able to do the task on our own. In some fields, this is called apprenticing or mentoring; in education, we call it scaffolding.

We can view learning on a continuum that begins with teacher modeling, where the student observes what he or she is supposed to learn, and ends with working independently, where the student performs the learned task accurately and efficiently on his or her own. Scaffolding happens in the gulf between modeling and working independently. Figure 3.1 shows the continuum of learning to read, from modeling to working independently.

Oral reading can be used as a scaffolding tool to ease the transition from modeling to independence. I call this "assisted reading" because the reading of a more proficient reader assists or supports the developing or struggling reader. The more proficient reader provides and gradually releases support as

Figure 3.1

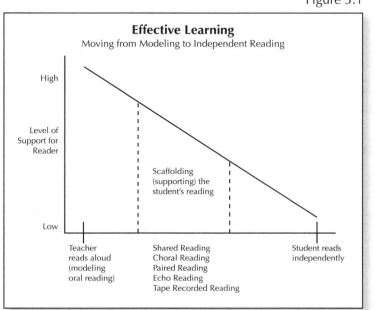

the less proficient reader becomes increasingly independent. Eventually, the less proficient student achieves full independence when he or she is able to perform the task accurately and efficiently without support. Assisted reading, which is sometimes called "oral support reading" or "reading while listening," has a well-established research base, especially for students who struggle in word recognition, fluency, or comprehension due to problems related to word recognition and fluency (Kuhn & Stahl, 2000; Rasinski & Hoffman, 2003; Sindelar, Monda, & O'Shea, 1990).

Assisted reading can take a variety of forms. For example, you can transform read aloud, a form of modeled reading, into shared reading, a form of oral assisted reading, by showing students the text and having them follow along silently as you read to them orally (Fountas & Pinnell, 1996, 2001). Paired reading, in which a student orally reads the same text with a more proficient partner, is another form of assisted reading.

In all forms of oral assisted reading, there is a minimum of two readers who read the same text aloud. The learner listens to a more proficient partner while simultaneously reading the text on his or her own. As the learner becomes more adept at that task, the partner gradually releases the support until the student can read the text independently.

In this chapter, I describe ways you can use oral assisted reading to provide an assist or scaffolding for students in grade 1 and beyond to move them toward independence and fluency in reading. These ideas are particularly helpful for struggling readers who have yet to achieve a level of independence that is essential to their progress in reading. In Chapter 6, I describe how assisted reading can play a significant role in instructional routines.

➤ Implementing Assisted Reading

Assisted reading comes in a variety of effective forms. The ones you choose depend on your style of teaching and the needs of your students. Nearly any type of text can be used for assisted reading. As you encounter books, magazines, and other materials, ask yourself how you might use them for a particular form of assisted reading. For some forms, such as paired reading, consider allowing students to choose the text.

Assisted reading can also be done in a variety of settings—as part of a direct instructional routine, during independent reading time, as a center activity, as an opening activity at the beginning of the day or right after lunch, as an end-of-the-day activity, during read aloud, as a home involvement program, as an essential part of a summer reading program, and so on.

Choral Reading

Choral reading, where groups of children read the same text aloud, is one of the most common forms of reading in the primary grades. It is a great way to maximize the amount of reading done per child. (Twenty children reading a 20-line page of text in unison certainly results in more reading per child than one child reading one line of the text, one at a time!)

Choral reading is also a wonderful way to build community in the classroom. For example, each morning as students read and recite the Pledge of Allegiance, they are declaring their unity as a community of learners. This routine also provides support for those students who are not yet fluent readers.

In Carol Tesh's third-grade class, students read chorally at least one new poem, song, or other lyrical text each day, as well as several familiar texts they've previously read. Carol writes the poems and songs on chart paper so that all students can see the text and invites children to read the words on their own at various times during the day: at the opening of the school day, before morning

Choral reading is a wonderful way to build class unity and maximize student reading.

recess, at transition times, after lunch, and before the end of the day. According to Carol, "Coming together to read in unison throughout the day reinforces the fact that we are a team and we need to work together, whether it's in reading, in writing, on the playground, or wherever."

Carol has noticed that during choral reading, even her most severe strugglers can read. "They seem to get the cue from the other readers in the class. We'll read a poem once, twice, three times a day or even more. And each time we read, their voices get stronger and more confident. Even the children who have the most difficult time in reading can read by the third time through. After listening to their classmates read, and then reading while listening to their classmates read, many struggling students come up to me near the end of the day and read the poem out loud on their own." Clearly, these students are benefiting from the support of Carol and their classmates.

David Paige (2008, 2009) studied the use of whole-class choral reading in middle school classrooms in an urban school district. Students chorally read a different passage each day (less than five minutes per day) from the district-mandated science textbook or a narrative passage from the district-mandated literature book. The choral reading appeared to be particularly helpful for improving the reading performance of struggling readers. Students themselves thought that the choral reading was a good way to practice reading because it allowed them the opportunity to read aloud with support from the teacher without suffering peer ridicule.

Types of Choral Reading

Typically, in choral reading, the entire group reads (or sings) one text completely and in unison. As the group reads, members may point to the words in the text to help track them visually. Alternative forms of choral reading (Vacca, Vacca, & Gove, 2000) are discussed below.

Refrain

In refrain choral reading, one student reads most of the text, and the whole group chimes in to read key segments chorally. The song read by the mother in Robert Munsch's *Love You Forever* is a fine example of refrain. The first and last stanza of Robert Service's poem "The Cremation of Sam McGee" is a good choice for refrain reading as well. Refrains should be written in large print on a chart, chalkboard, whiteboard, or smartboard and read and performed as a class.

Line-a-Child

In line-a-child choral reading, each child (or groups of two or three students) reads individually one or two lines of a text, usually from a rhyme or a poem, and the whole group reads the final line or lines together. The classic rhyme "One, Two, Buckle My Shoe" and the poem "Good Books, Good Times!" by Lee Bennett Hopkins (see Chapter 2, pages 54–55) are perfect to use for line-a-child.

Dialogue

Dialogue is similar to readers' theater, which is described in Chapter 5 on pages 117–130. Texts that work best for this form of choral reading contain different speaking parts, such as "Pussy Cat, Pussy Cat":

Narrator:	Pussy cat, pussy cat, where have you been?
Cat:	I've been to London to see the Queen.
Narrator:	Pussy cat, pussy cat, what did you do there?
Cat:	I frightened a little mouse under the chair.

One student or a portion of the class would read the part of the narrator, and another would read the part of the cat.

Antiphonal Reading

See antiphonal reading in action on the DVD.

For this version of choral reading, divide the whole class into groups (e.g., boys and girls; rows 1, 2, and 3) and assign a section of a text to each group. Then have one of the groups read its section while the rest of the class follows along silently. Other groups read other sections, usually the chorus or refrain. A variation of antiphonal reading is to have an individual read. Individual students read some sections, and groups of students read other sections.

Call and Response

In call and response, one student reads a line or two of a text, and the rest of the class responds by repeating the lines or reading the next few lines or the refrain. Song lyrics and historical documents such as the Declaration of Independence are good choices for call-and-response reading.

Echo Choral Reading

As the name implies, in echo reading you read one sentence or phrase at a time, and the student echoes back the same sentence or phrase, following the words with his or her finger so that you can be sure that the child is actually reading and not simply mimicking you.

On other occasions, especially with texts that the student can read with some degree of fluency, you might want to have him or her take the lead. Although not supported during reading, the student feels empowered and responsible as he or she models good reading and monitors your reading. Of course, if the student requires your support while reading, you should be ready to offer it. Echo reading provides a means for you to vary the level of support you provide, as there is a gradual release of responsibility from the teacher to the student.

Echo reading was included as part of a multistep intervention program for first-grade students called Peer-Assisted Literacy Strategies (PALS) (Mathes, Torgesen, & Allor, 2001). Low-achieving students receiving the PALS intervention (including the echo reading component) over 16 weeks made significant and substantial gains in reading achievement over first graders receiving more typical grade-level instruction.

Cumulative Choral Reading

In this form of choral reading, an individual or a small group reads one line or section of a passage. Another reader chimes in for the next line, and a few more readers for the lines that follow. By the time the end of the text is reached, the entire class should be reading. Certain texts, such as the Preamble to the Constitution of the United States, are well suited to a cumulative choral reading. The reading begins with one or two students reading "We the people. . . ." By the end of the Preamble, the entire class reads "do ordain and establish this constitution for the United States of America." This layering of voices can be inspiring because it brings to life the notion of "we the people."

Cumulative choral reading works in the other direction as well, with the whole class reading at first. With each succeeding line, one or more voices drop out. By the end of the text, only one or two students should be reading.

Choral Singing

See choral singing in action on the DVD.

A variation of choral reading is choral singing, which offers the same benefits as the other forms of choral reading mentioned earlier, and more. It is an excellent way to introduce beginning readers to written text because once students have memorized the lyrics, you can read them as a text, separate from the melody. From there, you can break lyrics down into individual lines, phrases, and then into words. Words can be broken into letters and patterns for building decoding skills. The goal is to get students to the point where they can recognize the words without the support of the melody or other contextual elements of the text.

Impromptu Choral Reading

Finally, imagine a group of three or four readers standing in front of an audience reading a poem aloud. The reading begins in a standard way with one student reading a line, but then it moves in an unpredictable fashion. One student reads some lines. Other lines are read by groups of two, three, or more students. All students read some lines. And, at various points in the reading, some students emphasize particular words. This is impromptu choral reading and, although it may seem chaotic, it can make for an impressive and compelling performance.

In impromptu choral reading, each reader essentially chooses whatever line, word, or phrase that he or she would like to read. In my experience, students tend to choose lines that have a strong emotional impact or contain content that is essential to understanding the piece. During the performance, some lines are read by individuals and others by groups of varying size. If nobody chooses a passage, which rarely happens, at least one reader always jumps in to save the performance. Impromptu choral reading is empowering for students, and it adds even greater variety to the list of choral reading possibilities.

Tips for Choosing Choral Reading Texts

- Remember that almost any text can be read chorally.
- Match the type of text you choose to a specific form of choral reading.
- Look for shorter texts that have good rhythm and distinct parts, such as poems, song lyrics, short stories, and toasts.
- Use texts that have a community value, such as the Pledge of Allegiance, the Preamble to the Constitution, inspirational poetry, and patriotic poems and songs.

Before attempting these forms of choral reading, allow time for planning and practice. Be sure to look over the text and ask yourself what form of choral reading would work best with it. Once students have become familiar and comfortable with the various forms of choral reading, they can choose a form that best fits a particular poem and their own style of performing. Then, be sure to practice the piece several times with your students before performing it for an audience. The practice itself is a wonderful way to build fluency and proficiency in reading. (See Chapters 4 and 5 for more on repeated reading and performance reading.)

Neurological Impress Method

Neurological Impress Method is a form of assisted oral reading that has some similarities with choral reading (Heckelman, 1969). In NIM, a student reads orally and simultaneously with a partner who acts as a tutor. Ideally, the text is at the student's instructional reading level and relates to a personal interest or school subject. The more proficient partner, reading slightly faster and louder than the student, makes a conscious effort to direct his or her voice into the student's left ear to "imprint" a sound-symbol match in his or her head. Reading one-on-one this way can be intense for students, so initial NIM sessions should be kept to just a few minutes. Even over time, most sessions should last no longer than 15 minutes.

Research into NIM (Heckelman, 1969) reports some spectacular gains. One student, for example, made a gain in reading of nearly six grade levels after doing NIM with a tutor for seven and a quarter hours over a six-week period (approximately five 15-minute sessions per week for six weeks). Twenty-four students made an average gain of nearly two grades levels over the same period of time.

Paired Reading

Paired reading is essentially a form of choral reading done by a pair of readers, usually one more proficient than the other. To me, it is a friendlier version of Neurological Impress Method reading. Rather than reading into someone's ear, in paired reading students (or mentor and student) read together side by side, with one gently "pushing" the other along. It is also known as "duolog reading" to distinguish it from other forms of partner reading, such as buddy reading, in which students alternate lines, paragraphs, or pages. The pair can be made up of the following groupings:

- parent and child
- teacher and child
- teacher aide or classroom volunteer and child

- older student and child
- two children at the same grade level, where there is some differential in reading proficiency

Paired reading was first described and used by Keith Topping (1987a, 1987b, 1989) as a form of tutoring between parent and child. However, he and others found that it could be easily adapted for other purposes, including classroom instruction.

Carrying out Paired Reading

Try to make paired reading a daily activity in your classroom for at least six consecutive weeks, with each session lasting from 10 to 20 minutes. Start by having the student choose the reading material. It might be something the child is reading on his or her own for pleasure or as a class assignment. As with any direct-teaching activity, the greatest gain will occur when the difficulty of the material is at the student's instructional level (i.e., 90 to 95 percent accuracy in word recognition)—neither too hard nor too easy, just right! See page 182 for guidelines on determining whether the text is at the student's instructional level.

Sit side by side in a comfortable chair that allows for good posture. Read together in a natural, comfortable manner, eyes focused directly on the text as one person (usually the student or the student who needs more help) follows along with a finger. Adjust your reading rate to match or gently "push" the student. You will also need to adjust your voice to match the demands of the text and the needs of the student. For example, if a portion of the text seems a bit difficult for the student, read in a somewhat louder voice and give the student more salient verbal cues. Once the student is reading successfully, tone down your voice so that it provides a lighter level of support.

If the student makes a decoding error while reading, simply state the correct pronunciation of the word while pointing at it, ask the student to do the same, and move on. Paired reading is not the time to stop and begin a decoding lesson, which would only interrupt fluency and meaning. Rather, you may wish to make a mental note of the miscued words and chat with the student about them after the session—how the words are pronounced, what cues in the words help us with pronunciation, what the words mean, and so forth.

When the student feels confident reading a portion of the text on his or her own, he or she should give you a prearranged "solo" signal, such as a gentle elbow nudge to your side. This gives the student control over the paired reading experience. At this point, you should stop reading aloud, but continue to read silently and monitor the student's reading. If the student runs into trouble, immediately resume reading orally. The student may also signal you to resume oral reading even if he or she isn't experiencing difficulty. If the student needs a brief break, you can read orally, while he or she reads silently or in a whisper. Before the reading, be sure to agree on a signal for this, too. (An elbow to a different location usually works well.) At the end of the paired reading, be sure to chat about the meaning of the passage and how the actual reading went.

It's a good idea to keep track of paired reading sessions, whether they occur in the classroom or at home between parent and child. Figures 3.2 and 3.3, respectively, illustrate a completed record-keeping sheet and a blank sheet that you can use. Figures 3.4 and 3.5 provide a blank sheet and a completed response sheet for giving feedback to students.

I have also included a set of directions for doing paired reading (see Figure 3.6), to share with parents, volunteers, or students who may need guidelines.

The Benefits of Paired Reading

Does paired reading work? The research has shown extraordinarily positive results. In one study of paired reading over a period of six to ten weeks, for example, students made gains of at least six months in reading (Limbrick, McNaughton, & Cameron, 1985). In other studies (Topping, 1989), students made gains that were approximately three times greater than expected. (One month gain for one month of instruction is normally expected. The students in this study made at least three months gain for every month of paired reading.) Paired reading has been found to work with students from primary school to high school. Moreover, Topping (1989) reports that the students who worked as teachers or tutors for other students also made substantial gains in reading.

In addition to the results of quantitative research, the testimony of teachers needs to be counted. Sue Gump, Mary Lu Ramsey, and Jackie Orosz, remedial reading teachers at elementary and middle schools, have used paired reading in parent-child tutoring programs and report great success. Jackie, who is also trained in Reading Recovery, claims that paired reading and Reading Recovery "are the best things to have happened in remedial reading programs" (Rasinski & Fredericks, 1991, p. 515).

Figure 3.2

Paired Reading Record Sheet

Name: __Jenny R._____ Week of: ___November 18___

Day	# Minutes Read	Partner	Book/Text Read	Comments
Monday	15	Mom	Social Studies Book	Difficult material to read. Prepped for test.
Tuesday	10	Mom	Tuck Everlasting	Jenny did a super job!
Wednesday	10	Mom	Tuck Everlasting	
Thursday	10	Mom	Tuck Everlasting	Great book!
Friday	--	--	--	Went to birthday party!
Saturday	15	Dad	Tuck Everlasting	
Sunday	10	Dad	Newspaper	Read headline article

Please return this form to your teacher every Monday morning.

Scholastic Teaching Resources *The Fluent Reader*

A completed Paired Reading Record Sheet

Paired Reading Record Sheet

Figure 3.3

Name:_____ Week of:_____

Day	# Minutes Read	Partner	Book/Text Read	Comments
Monday				
Tuesday				
Wednesday				
Thursday				
Friday				
Saturday				
Sunday				

Please return this form to your teacher every Monday morning.

Scholastic Teaching Resources *The Fluent Reader*

Figure 3.4

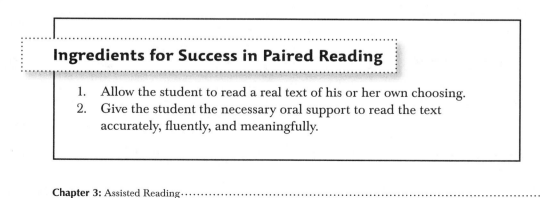

Paired Reading Response Form

Student: __Michael__   Partner: __Mrs. Kelly__

Date: __November 12__

Text Read	Minutes Read	Feedback
Mr. Popper's Penguins	15	You did a great job! I loved how you were willing to try to read on your own. You're reading with better expression and phrasing.

When reading independently.

	1 Needs Improvement	3 OK	5 Doing Great

Rate/pacing __2__

Phrasing __3__

Expression __3__

Decoding __4__

Scholastic Teaching Resources   *The Fluent Reader*

A completed Paired Reading Response Form

Ingredients for Success in Paired Reading

1. Allow the student to read a real text of his or her own choosing.
2. Give the student the necessary oral support to read the text accurately, fluently, and meaningfully.

Paired Reading Response Form

Figure 3.5

Student: _____   **Partner:** _____

Date: _____

Text Read	Minutes Read	Feedback

When reading
independently.

	1	3	5
	Needs Improvement	OK	Doing Great

Rate/pacing _____

Phrasing _____

Expression _____

Decoding _____

Figure 3.6

Paired Reading: A Quick Guide

Paired reading is an activity shared by two readers, one stronger than the other. It works best with students who are experiencing difficulty with decoding and general fluency. Follow these steps:

1. Do paired reading at least five times per week, 10 to 20 minutes per session, for at least six consecutive weeks.
2. Allow the student to choose the material to read. Pleasure reading or school assignments are equally acceptable.
3. Find a comfortable, quiet place to sit side by side. Position the text so that it can be easily viewed by both readers.
4. If the text is a continuation of a previous day's reading, quickly review what was read.
5. Begin reading together. Adjust your intonation and rate to the student's level of proficiency. Read with a distinct and expressive voice that is slightly faster than the student would normally read on his or her own.
6. Have the student follow the text with a finger as you both read.
7. If the student makes an error (or hesitates for a few seconds on a word), wait to see if he or she corrects it. If there is no self-correction, pronounce the word and have the student repeat it. Then continue reading. Review and discuss errors at the end of the session.
8. Decide on a nonverbal signal with the student (e.g., a gentle elbow nudge to your side) that indicates that he or she wants to read independently. When such a signal is given, you should either stop reading aloud or read in a whisper that "shadows" the student's reading.
   a. If the student encounters difficulty during solo reading, provide help and resume reading aloud.
   b. If the student wishes to read independently again later, he or she should use the agreed-upon signal.
9. At the end of the session, chat with the student about the reading behaviors that are improving. Praise his or her efforts. Talk about any particularly difficult words or portions of the text. Discuss the meaning of the text.
10. Complete the Paired Reading Record Sheet and the Paired Reading Response Form. (See Figures 3.3 and 3.5.)

Audio Recorded Reading

If you think paired reading or Neurological Impress Method reading is a good idea but don't have volunteers in the classroom, adequate support from home, or enough time for yourself to make it happen, try recorded reading. Give students books and other reading materials on audiotape or a CD and allow them to listen on their own while reading a print version of the text.

Carol Chomsky (1976) worked with an approach for teaching reading that involved the assisted and repeated reading of texts. Chomsky asked struggling readers to practice reading passages while simultaneously listening to audio-recorded versions of the same passage read fluently until the students could read the passage without assistance. Students in this intervention made remarkable progress not only on the passages they practiced but also on new passages they'd never before read. Moreover, Chomsky reported that students demonstrated improvements in their confidence in and attitude toward reading.

Marie Carbo calls her adaptation of this approach "talking books" and has employed it with struggling readers for several years. She demonstrated that students who read aloud a book while listening to it on tape made strong gains in reading (1978a, 1978b, 1981), well beyond what she expected based on their previous progress in reading. In one study from New Zealand (Smith & Elley, 1997), students who read and listened repeatedly to high-interest stories on tape until they felt they could read them successfully on their own made an average gain of 2.2 years in reading achievement, after participating in the study for about 27 weeks, or three-quarters of a school year. That's three times the gain expected of normally developing readers, yet these students were struggling! Moreover, students who participated in this study maintained their gain over the course of a two-month summer break. Students who couldn't read fluently were able to do so, with the help of stories on tape.

Other studies have found that giving audio-recorded reading materials to English language learners (ELL), students for whom English is not their first language (Koskinen et. al, 1999), for independent practice holds great promise. In the Koskinen study, most ELL students reported that they practiced almost daily reading with the books and tapes. Moreover, the least proficient ELL readers were most likely to use the pre-recorded materials to practice and improve their reading at home.

When assigning recorded readings, be sure to remind students to read the text (track the words visually) as they listen. Otherwise they will gain very little from the activity. If students are not following along visually, they may enjoy listening to the material read to them, but since they are not actually reading, little if any growth in reading will occur.

Buddy Reading

Fourth-grade teacher Lorraine Griffith was concerned that many of her students were not actually reading during sustained silent reading (SSR) time, but rather were just browsing through books they selected, chatting with friends, or were otherwise off task. So, recognizing that reading is largely a social activity, she replaced SSR with a buddy reading program.

In buddy reading, students at similar reading levels are paired up for about 20 to 30 minutes per session. Each pair chooses a book or other reading material. From there, students negotiate how they will orally read the text together. Some pairs alternate pages, others read chorally, as in paired reading, some read and reread one page at a time in echo fashion, and others try a combination of methods.

Lorraine encourages pairs to stop reading periodically, talk about what they have read, and ask questions of each other—especially when one student is having difficulty understanding the text. At the end of the session, buddies determine which pages in their shared book they will read at home that night, so they continue the reading silently and independently. Moreover, coordinating home reading makes each student feel responsible to his or her partner.

Buddy reading can be an excellent alternative to sustained silent reading (SSR).

Lorraine feels that buddy reading leads to more reading, both in school and at home. "It really helps students see that reading is a social activity and creates some continuity between school and home reading." She also feels that it helps her keep track of her students' reading and engage in more meaningful reading conferences. "When I hear them reading aloud, I have a better sense of the content they are covering, and it is easier for me to chat with them about their books."

➤ Concluding Thoughts

Oral assisted reading allows you to do something that silent reading doesn't: provide tangible, direct, and online support to the student as he or she reads. The learning process begins with the teacher having full responsibility for the task: The teacher models what is to be learned. In reading, modeling happens when we read a text to students and, perhaps, describe our thinking and our reading along the way. Little by little, however, the teacher asks the student to take on more responsibility for the reading.

As time goes on, the student takes a more active role in the reading, and the teacher reduces his or her support. In the end, ideally, the student is able to read independently. He or she is not only successful on practice texts, but on new, unfamiliar texts as well. The learning that occurs during assisted reading—learning to decode words, to read with expression, to construct meaning from connected text—transfers. The gradual release of support and responsibility from the teacher to the student is at the heart of successful literacy instruction.

Oral reading makes the reading process transparent for the teacher and student. It puts the process "on the table" to be observed, examined, supported, and practiced until independence is achieved. When we employ the forms of oral assisted reading described in this chapter, even with challenging texts, the student will succeed.

Where to Find Audio Recorded Materials

Audio Recorded Texts You can purchase pre-recorded books from sources such as teacher stores and Scholastic Book Clubs. However, I have found it most effective to create my own. In doing so, I can adjust my reading rate to match the reading rate of my students. In fact, I sometimes record the same text at a slow and a normal rate and use them sequentially to move the reader to independence.

In some schools, upper-elementary teachers have their students create recorded versions of books for primary students—for example, third graders make books for first graders, fourth graders for second graders, and fifth graders for third graders. The recordings and printed books are sent to their designated recipients, who benefit from listening to and reading them—but it's not only the younger students who benefit. Since the older students are not allowed to record their books until they can read them with good expression and at an appropriate rate, they need to practice their reading several times. (As you will see in Chapter 4, practiced reading, or repeated reading, is another key to successful reading development.) Moreover, this activity puts just-right materials into the hands of struggling upper-grade students. Making recordings for younger schoolmates is a natural way to get those students reading easier books—books at their instructional level—without making them feel embarrassed or frustrated.

Podcasts The advent of podcasting has made recording books and other texts even easier. A podcast is nothing more than an audio recording. However, rather than recording one's voice using a tape recorder and cassette tapes, the recording is done on the computer on an electronic file that can be easily stored in the memory of the computer or other electronic memory device. The recording can be played on a computer, or on an iPod/MP3 device, and it can also be sent and distributed electronically to students and families via e-mail. The possibilities for students (and teachers) to create podcasts of written texts for others to read and listen to (engage in assisted reading) are endless. Information on how to create podcasts can be found at the following Web site: http://computer.howstuff-works.com/podcasting3.htm. You can find podcasts I've created on the DVD and at www.teachercreatedmaterials.com/podcasts.

Video Recordings Video recordings are available that present familiar children's songs and lyrics. As students listen to the song, they can read and sing along to the lyrics, which run along the bottom of the screen as captions. Visuals often include some sort of related animation, as well. Once students become fluent in reading the lyrics on the screen, you can move them toward more independent forms of reading. You might print the song's lyrics, individual lines, and words on paper, sentence strips, and word cards and have students practice them without the recording. Going from high support to low support to independence in reading illustrates the gradual release of responsibility that we need to follow in our instruction.

Captioned Videos Because captioned television and other captioned video presentations show printed text being read along with the oral production of the text, they can also be used as a form of assisted oral reading. Studies reported by Koskinen and her colleagues (1993) and Postlethwaite and Ross (1992) point to their effectiveness. It is often difficult for many of us to keep our eyes off the text when watching captioned television—psychologists call this an obligatory process. I have found evidence of this when watching captioned television with adults and children—and the spelling errors prove it. When the captions contain errors, my viewing mates and I always notice and call them out. If your eyes are drawn to the print while watching captioned television, think of the possibilities for helping developing and struggling readers who often read little but watch plenty of TV.

~ *Chapter 4* ~
Repeated Reading
Practice Makes Perfect in Reading

"Reading is to the mind what exercise is to the body."
—Sir Richard Steele

So far, we've explored two ways to help students become proficient, expressive, and meaningful readers: by modeling that kind of reading through read aloud (Chapter 2) and by providing students with oral assistance (Chapter 3) as they read. We can also help students by giving them opportunities to practice oral reading.

▶Wide Versus Deep Practice in Reading

Applying basic skills automatically is usually achieved through practice. Normally, in reading education, we associate practice with wide reading—the kind of reading most adults and children do. We read a book, newspaper article, or other reading selection, and when we are finished, we move on to another book, article, or selection. This form of reading practice is, appropriately, the foundation for all reading instruction and is the centerpiece for most core reading programs.

However, for some students—generally younger and struggling readers—wide reading is not enough. When these students read a passage a first time, their reading is not good; at best, it's mediocre. If these students engage solely in wide reading, they will be going from one mediocre reading to another. Is it any wonder why these students continually struggle in reading and have such difficulty in moving toward more proficient reading?

Again, for these students, wide reading is not enough. They also need to read deeply. By deep reading, I mean reading one text (or a portion of a longer text) several times through until it can be read proficiently and fluently—with few errors, appropriate rate, meaningful expression, and good comprehension. The repeated practice of reading one passage allows students to develop mastery over a given text before they move to another piece.

Repeated practice finds its way into many of life's endeavors. Athletes, for example, often talk about doing a certain number of "reps" to perfect a particular move. Perhaps your mother can bake a cake from scratch or cook a turkey without consulting a cookbook. She probably achieved that level of proficiency in her culinary skills by observing someone else skilled at baking and cooking, working closely with that person during the initial stages of her learning, and having plenty of opportunities to put those particular skills to good use. After a time, she was essentially able to perform her culinary magic without the assistance of a coach or cookbook. Basketball players practice jump shots and foul shots daily, so that the movements necessary for making those shots become second nature or automatic. Musicians practice or rehearse new compositions so that when they're on the stage they can focus on the subtle aspects of performance, such as tone, emphasis, and phrasing, rather than the written score itself.

I recently had the opportunity to interview some highly skilled musicians. I asked why they needed to rehearse a new composition they were to perform even though their initial playing of the piece sounded very good to my untrained ear. They told me that although their initial performance of the piece might sound good, they were visually "glued" to the sheet music. Being members of an orchestra, they needed to rehearse the composition so that they could come visually "unglued" from the sheet music. Doing so would allow them to keep their eyes on the conductor, stay in time and tempo with the other members of the orchestra, and attend to those more subtle aspects of their performance. In other words, the musicians needed to rehearse so that their minds could go from the mechanics of their performance to those higher levels. In reading, we want students to come "unglued" from the words themselves so that their minds can go to a higher level—comprehension, or paying attention to meaning.

Word decoding is a basic skill in reading, one that is absolutely essential to success. Not only must students be able to decode words and phrases with a high degree of accuracy, they must also be able to decode them automatically, with minimal attention or effort. Practice through repeated reading helps them get there.

➤The Benefits of Repeated Reading

When we become fluent at a task, we can devote our attention to other related tasks. For basketball, related tasks might include watching the clock and being mindful of opposing players. For cooking, related tasks might include the preparation of many dishes simultaneously. And in reading, the most significant related task is comprehension. Through practice, the reader's decoding can become so fluent that he or she pays minimum attention to the words and maximum attention to creating meaning from the words encountered.

The theory of automaticity supports this idea (LaBerge & Samuels, 1974). In one test of the theory, Samuels (1979) asked students experiencing severe learning difficulties to read orally a short passage several times. With each practice reading of the passage, the students read with greater accuracy, speed, and comprehension. This, of course, is expected; you get better at what you practice. Samuels observed another effect, however. As students mastered certain passages, they were given other passages of equal or greater difficulty. Samuels found that students' first readings of the new passage were actually better than their initial readings of the previous passage. Moreover, it took fewer practices to achieve a set goal.

Practice, therefore, not only led to improvements in the reading of the familiar passage, but also of passages the students had not previously seen. As students became more fluent in their reading of one passage, their improved reading at both the word and sentence level transferred to new passages. Samuels described this effect in terms of the theory of automaticity.

A series of follow-up studies have confirmed the efficacy of repeated readings as a powerful instructional tool (Rasinski, Reutzel, Chard, & Linan-Thompson, in press). Indeed, in her review of research on repeated reading, Sarah Dowhower (1989) identifies the following key proven benefits of the method:

- Repeated reading helps good and poor readers recall facts from their reading. It also aids good readers in focusing on and remembering higher-level, important information. Studies have found that improvements in comprehension extend to unpracticed passages for primary through middle-grade students (Dowhower, 1987; Morgan & Lyon, 1979; Rasinski, Reutzel, Chard, & Linan-Thompson, in press).

In the Morgan and Lyon study, for example, struggling readers in junior high made gains of more than eleven months on a standardized comprehension test in slightly over six months of repeated reading instruction. Considering that struggling readers, by definition, make less than a month's gain for a month's worth of instruction, these gains are impressive. Improvements in comprehension are particularly strong when students are encouraged to reread for meaning, not speed (O'Shea & Sindelar, 1983).

- Repeated reading is an excellent study strategy, equal to or better than other more complex and cumbersome strategies such as note taking, outlining, summarizing, or recalling information.
- Repeated reading helps students remember important information—such as main ideas and important vocabulary—in technical and unfamiliar material and results in improved problem solving (Bromage & Mayer, 1986; Mayer, 1983).
- Repeated reading results in improved story comprehension and leads to more sophisticated questioning and insights when a text is presented as a "repeated read aloud" (a combination of read aloud and repeated readings) (Martinez & Roser, 1985).
- Repeated reading promotes more efficient (faster) reading with greater word recognition accuracy (Carver & Hoffman, 1981; Chomsky, 1976; Dahl, 1974; Dowhower, 1987; Herman, 1985; Neill, 1980; Rashotte & Torgesen, 1985; Samuels, 1979). Although comprehension is central to successful reading, quick, accurate, and automatic processing of text is important, too; it is a perquisite for comprehension (Rasinski, 2000, 2006). A student who reads a text passage at a rate of 140 words per minute and with excellent comprehension is clearly superior to one who reads the same text with the same level of understanding but at a rate of 60 words per minute. If we accept the notion that the more one reads, the better

reader one becomes (Postlethwaite & Ross, 1992), then faster and more efficient processing of text results in more reading over time. Rather than focusing on speed and accuracy as distinct elements in reading, I prefer to combine the concepts under the notion of automaticity or efficiency in text processing.

- Repeated reading helps struggling readers break out of word-by-word reading to read with more meaningful phrasing (Dowhower, 1987).

To these benefits identified by Dowhower, I would add one more:

- Although repeated reading is often viewed by students as a mechanical and somewhat boring task, it can be an authentic, engaging, and enjoyable activity for them. When students are given real reasons to engage in practice (e.g., to eventually perform for an audience), they are often more than willing to rehearse. If they rehearse and perform well, they can become the stars of their classroom!

➤ Implementing Repeated Reading Through Direct Instruction

There are a variety of ways to implement repeated reading in the classroom. In the remainder of this chapter, I show how repeated reading can be used in direct and intensive ways to help students struggling with reading in general and reading fluency in particular. In Chapter 5, I offer authentic ways to use repeated readings with all students.

Thomas and Erin had just completed third grade and were enrolled in our university's reading clinic. Both children had been experiencing significant reading difficulties. They read in a slow, monotone, and labored manner, and with little enthusiasm. Moreover, the two children could recall little of what they had read. And because Thomas and Erin had experienced little success in reading, they had begun to dislike and avoid it.

Claudia, a reading clinic teacher, used repeated readings to help Thomas and Erin improve their fluency and comprehension. She introduced an age-appropriate poem daily to the children, reading it aloud and talking about it with them. Then she, Thomas, and Erin read the poem chorally several times through, with the children pointing to the text as they read. After a few choral readings, Thomas and Erin recorded their own reading on a tape recorder. The children took the print and recorded versions of the poem home to practice and improve on their recorded performance. When the children returned the next day, they were invited to read the poem to Claudia, me, and a few other adults. The improvement in the students' reading was amazing. They read with accuracy and expression, and their overall reading had improved significantly. In just five weeks, both students made over a year's gain in fluency and overall reading achievement. Equally important, we noticed a distinct change in their attitudes toward reading: Thomas and Erin knew that with practice they could become "Reading Idols!" In some cases, especially for those students experiencing severe difficulty in reading, a direct approach is often best.

Guidelines for Repeated Reading

Below are guidelines for implementing repeated reading for those students you think would benefit from it the most.

Preparation

1. Set aside 15 to 30 minutes per day for repeated reading instruction.
2. Choose reading passages between 50 and 500 words. These passages may come from a variety of sources—basal readers, textbooks, trade books, poetry anthologies, newspapers, or student writing. I have found that texts that have a strong voice and are meant to be performed are ideally suited for repeated reading. The rhythmic nature and brevity of poetry and song lyrics, for example, make them easy to learn and fun to perform. The length of the texts to be read depends on the age and ability of the reader. As students become more proficient, they can begin to take on longer and more complex passages.
3. Determine the difficulty level of the passages by following the guidelines in Figure 4.1 on page 94. But remember that these measurements are only estimates. See how the passage "fits" the individual reader. If it's on the difficult side, provide oral reading assistance in the initial repeated readings by reading the passage with the student. If it's on the easy side, don't worry about providing the extra support. Expect the student to achieve the criterion level rather quickly. Think about develop-

ing and organizing a collection of passages at a variety of levels to use as your students' skills improve. This a good project for a summer vacation!

Procedure

1. Sit next to the child in a comfortable, quiet location.
2. Choose a passage and make sure it is at or near the student's instructional reading level, which means that, upon a first oral reading of a passage, he or she exhibits 85 to 95 percent word recognition accuracy. If a student reads a passage closer to the 85 percent accuracy level or reads with excessive slowness (less than 50 words per minute), you may need to offer oral assisted reading, such as reading along with the student, in the initial repeated reading. (For more information on assisted reading, see Chapter 3.) Or you may wish to choose an easier passage.
3. Have the student orally practice an appropriate passage until he or she has achieved the criterion reading rate on the passage, using the guidelines in Figure 4.2 on page 95 to determine individual students' rates. These are typical end-of-year criterion levels for first grade and up (Hasbrouck & Tindal, 1992, 2006). But feel free to adapt levels for your own students and your instructional goals and their instructional needs.

Grade Level	Target Number of Correct Words Per Minute
end of first grade	50
end of second grade	90
end of third grade	110
end of fourth grade	120
end of fifth grade	140
sixth grade and higher	150

4. Once students have achieved the target criterion level, assign a new passage that is as difficult as or slightly more difficult than the passage they just practiced.
5. Keep a log of the passages students are working on daily and the dates on which they master them. (See Figures 4.3 and 4.4 on pages 96 and 97.)

6. Track student progress by administering an oral reading probe weekly, biweekly, or monthly on passages the students have not previously read. (See Figure 4.3 and Chapter 8 for details.)

Figure 4.1

How to Determine the Difficulty Level of a Passage

Difficulty levels for texts are generally expressed in readability levels. A readability level is a number that indicates the passage's approximate grade-level equivalent—the grade at which most students should be able to read the passage with the teacher's help. Readability levels are usually determined using a formula that measures sentence difficulty and word difficulty. These formulas give, at best, rough estimates since they leave out the most important factor in determining reading difficulty: the individual reader. Nevertheless, they do provide an indication of difficulty. Here are two simple approaches for determining difficulty levels:

Word Processing Method
This method requires a word processing program. Simply type the target passage into a word processing program. Then on the Tools menu, look for and click on Readability, which is usually within the spelling and grammar checker (often under Preferences). The program will automatically determine the passage's readability in grade-level equivalents.

Web Site Method
Several Web sites contain programs that allow you to measure readability by simply entering a passage for which you wish to determine the readability level. Here are three of my favorites:
- SMOG Readability Formula:
  www.harrymclaughlin.com/SMOG.htm
- Spache Readability Formula (grades 1–3):
  www.interventioncentral.org/htmdocs/tools/okapi/okapi.php
- Dale-Chall Readability formula (grades 4+):
  www.interventioncentral.org/htmdocs/tools/okapi/okapi.php

Figure 4.2

How to Determine a Student's Reading Rate

There are two easy ways to determine a student's reading rate. For both methods, you will need a watch that allows you to measure seconds. *Tip:* Limit measures of rate to the number of words the student reads correctly (including words he or she self-corrects after an initial error).

One-Minute Reading Probe

Choose a target passage that is at the student's grade level and make a photocopy of it. Have the student read the passage aloud to you for one minute. If the student makes an error and does not self-correct it, draw a line through the word. If the student comes to a word that he or she is unable to decode or does not try to decode it, simply supply the word after a count of three and draw a line through it. (For formal names or unusual words, give credit if the student decodes them in a way that seems appropriate for his or her level of reading.) At the end of 60 seconds, have the student stop reading (or mark the 60-second point if you want the student to read the entire passage). Count the number of words read correctly to determine the student's words-per-minute reading rate. (For more detailed guidelines on administering a one-minute reading probe, see Chapter 8.)

Entire Text Method

Although this method takes longer, it makes for a more authentic reading experience because students read a piece of at least several paragraphs, from start to finish, as we do in the real world. To determine a student's reading rate using this method, figure out the number of seconds it takes him or her to read the entire passage. Count the number of words read correctly or self-corrected after an initial error. Insert those numbers into the following formula:

$$\frac{\#\ \text{words read correctly}}{\#\ \text{of seconds to read}} \times 60 = \text{reading rate in words correct per minute}$$

(Figure 4.2, continued)

Example: The passage is made up of 245 words. The student reads the passage in 134 seconds and makes 3 errors, so 242 words were read correctly.

$$\frac{242}{134} \times 60 = 108 \text{ words correct per minute (wcpm)}$$

Figure 4.3

Repeated Reading Log

Student: Kristi

Passage	Passage Reading Level	Probe 1		Probe 2		Probe 3		Probe 4		Comments
		Date	WCPM	Date	WCPM	Date	WCPM	Date	WCPM	
5th grade IRI Form A	5.0	9/16	80	9/17	102	9/19	105	9/20	110	Practiced several times on Mon & Tues
5th grade IRI Form B	5.0	9/23	87	9/24	100	9/25	104	9/27	120	Paired reading— read 3 times 9/26
5th grade IRI Form C	5.0	9/30	90	10/1	102	10/3	110	10/4	118	
Basal Reader page 88	5.2	10/8	86	10/9	94	10/10	112	10/11	122	Practiced at home 2X every night

A partially completed Repeated Reading Log

Repeated Reading Log

Figure 4.4

Student: _____

Passage	Passage Reading Level	Probe 1		Probe 2		Probe 3		Probe 4		Comments
		Date	WCPM	Date	WCPM	Date	WCPM	Date	WCPM	

Scholastic Teaching Resources   *The Fluent Reader*

Radio Reading

Radio reading (Greene, 1979; Opitz & Rasinski, 2008; Searfoss, 1975) is another form of repeated reading. It was developed as a more authentic and collaborative alternative to round robin reading, the archaic form of small-group instruction where the teacher chooses students to read aloud "on the spot" from an assigned text, without the benefit of practice. Round robin readings are often disfluent, inexpressive, uninspired, and filled with word recognition errors. Performances like these do little for the group's enjoyment of reading and even less for the reader's confidence in himself or herself. And since round robin reading is practiced regularly in many classrooms, the poor oral reading it engenders too often finds its way into other components of the literacy program such as guided reading.

In radio reading, as in round robin reading, groups of four to six students read aloud an assigned text. The difference is that the parts to be read are assigned the day before. (See Figure 4.5 on pages 100–101 for step-by-step guidelines on implementing radio reading.) I prefer to use passages from texts that the group has already read silently because students are familiar with the meaning and outcome of the text and can plan their presentation accordingly. If you use an unfamiliar text, be sure to provide students with a detailed overview of it before carrying out radio reading. When you use radio reading, ask students to think of themselves as radio or television announcers. They will need to practice the text in order to use their oral reading voice to convey meaning to the audience. Inform students that they will be performing the passage and asking questions about it.

When assigning parts, use good judgment based on what you know about your students as readers. Assign the longest or most challenging parts to those most able to handle them. You might also want to give a mini-lesson on the importance of reading with meaningful expression, just as radio and television announcers do. Emphasize that the only way to be able to read with good expression is through practice.

Ask each student to prepare two questions about his or her part—one literal (i.e., finding the answer requires the reader to look "right there" in the text) and one inferential (i.e., finding the answer requires the reader to "think and search" the text, using the information from the text, as well as his or her own background knowledge). Here are examples of each type of question:

> **Literal/"right there":** What was the name of the main
> character in my reading?
>
> **Inferential/"think and search":** Why did people dislike
> this character? What did he do, say, or stand for that made
> people hate him?

Once you've assigned a part to each student, have him or her practice
reading it aloud and repeatedly. Provide class time for individual practice and
cooperative repeated reading, which is explained on pages 103–104. Students can
also practice their reading and develop their questions at home.

On the next day, have students gather in their groups and present their
readings one by one, in the appropriate order according to the text. I sometimes ask students to come to the front of the group, stand tall, and read to the
group as if they were giving a formal presentation. On other occasions, I have
students simply read from their seats or choose a place from which they would
like to read.

Ask students to read as expressively and meaningfully as possible, as if they
were professional announcers. I find that a faux microphone on a stand or an old
radio is a good prop for reminding students of that point. If a student miscalls
a word, give him or her an opportunity to correct it. If the student can't, you
(not the other students) should provide the correct word and ask him or her to
continue, thus minimizing the disruption. The student may also call on you for
help with particular words or phrases. Again, supply the word or phrase and urge
the student to continue reading. As in paired reading, you may wish to make note
of words that give students difficulty. Those words can be the focus of a quick
mini-lesson after the radio reading session. The students who are not reading
should either read along silently (a form of assisted reading) in the book or listen
attentively with their books closed.

After all students have presented their parts, have them ask their literal and
inferential questions in a follow-up discussion. Encourage students to elaborate
on questions and responses, and find quotes from the text that illustrate or justify
their points. Questions you might ask students to help them elaborate include
the following:

- That's an interesting question. How did you come up with it?
- Tell us more about this character. Does he remind you of anyone you know or have read about?
- Can you find a section from the passage that gives us clues to answer that question?
- What do you think was the most interesting quote from today's reading? Why do you think so?
- How does this story compare with the one we read last week?

After the discussion, ask students to summarize the reading, their oral presentations, and what they need to work on in their oral reading and comprehension skills and strategies for their next radio reading session.

Teaching Tip: Record Radio Readings

Tape-record radio readings so that students can analyze them later. Save the very best recordings and play them as a model for future reading groups that are assigned the same text. Then, those groups can try to outperform the recorded performance!

Figure 4.5

Radio Reading: A Quick Guide

The Day Before Radio Reading
1. Choose a passage from your regular guided reading program, basal reader, or a trade book that is long enough to be read by four to six students. Choose a selection that has already been read silently, or, if the selection has not been read previously, give students a detailed overview of the selection.
2. Provide students with a mini-lesson on the importance of reading aloud with expression and meaning, using radio and television announcers as examples of people who do it well.
3. Assign parts of the passage to students. Give the most challenging parts to students who are best able to handle them. Assignments do not need to be equal in length.

4. Have students practice reading their parts orally, alone or with others, in school and at home.

5. Ask each student to develop two questions about his or her part: a literal, fact-based question, and an inferential question that requires students to use information from the text and their background knowledge to arrive at an answer.

The Day of Radio Reading

1. Remind students about the need to read with expression and meaning.

2. Provide props such as a microphone or radio to lend authenticity to the experience.

3. Have students read their assigned parts orally in the proper order.

4. If students encounter problems in their reading, provide help or allow them to call on you for help. Deal with the difficulty quickly to minimize disruption. (Remind students not to call out words that another student is having difficulty with. You will provide that assistance.)

5. After all the readings are complete, have students discuss the entire passage using the questions they prepared the day before.

6. At the end of the discussion, have students summarize the story, critique their reading, and make suggestions for the next radio reading.

Say It Like the Character

Oral reading fluency means more than reading accurately and quickly. It also involves reading with expression as a way to get at the text's meaning. In Say It Like the Character (Opitz & Rasinski, 2008), students get "inside" characters from books by reading monologues and dialogues orally. Listeners must make inferences about the characters

Students practice passages to improve their ability to read them with expression and meaning.

Units of study #2

through the way the passage was read. For this to happen, readers need to do two things: practice reading the assigned text (fluency), and think about the feelings and disposition of the character (comprehension).

To try Say It Like the Character, find passages that contain monologues or dialogues. They can be as short as a sentence or as long as a full page. Look in books that students are reading on their own or that you are reading to them. Make copies of the passages. If the story from which the passage comes is unfamiliar, give students some background so that they understand the events and emotions leading up to the passage. Have the students practice reading the passage silently as well as orally. Then read aloud a portion of it in several tones of voice (e.g., angry, delighted, confused, surprised) and talk about the feelings that can be inferred. A list of emotions by category is provided below. I know many teachers who have made a chart of selected emotions, posted it in their classrooms, and then made reference to the chart when asking students to choose an emotion to portray in their reading.

List of Emotions

Fear, Anxiety, Apprehensiveness, Worry
Anger, Displeasure, Hostility
Pride (an exaggerated positive evaluation of oneself)
Love (strong affection for another)
Happy, Optimistic (well-being, content)
Enthusiasm, Vitality (strong excitement)
Grief (intense sorrow, especially caused by someone's death)
Sad, Unhappy, Depressed, Sorrowful
Astonishment, Surprise (filled with sudden wonder or amazement)

Once students get the idea, have them try Say It Like the Character on their own with a new passage. You can assign them a feeling or an emotion to embed in their reading or let them choose their own. Have students practice the reading and then perform it, one at a time, in small groups. The students listening must guess the emotion that the reader is feeling. Following the reading, have students discuss what the reader did to convey the intended emotion (increased or decreased volume or pitch of voice, changed reading rate, paused dramatically, emphasized a particular word), as well as the markers in the text itself (italics, bold print, illustrations) that gave clues to what the character was feeling.

Poetry works well for Say It Like the Character, too. I often give two or more students the same poem to read aloud, along with an emotional context from which to develop their reading, such as "You just won the lottery" or "You just found out that your best friend is moving away." Students practice their reading at home and, the next day, present it. This becomes a dramatic example of how meaning is carried not only by words, but is also conveyed by the way that the words are presented by the reader.

Mary Person (1990) describes a variation on Say It Like the Character. She prints words for specific feelings on cards, such as fear, rage, sadness, excitement, and joy. She also prints a variety of sentences on sentence strips (e.g., "The children ran screaming down the hallway." "We were surprised to hear the knock on the door. Who could it be?") Each student chooses or is assigned one feeling card and one sentence strip, then reads the sentence in a way that captures the emotion on the card.

Mumble Reading

Mumble reading allows many students to do repeated readings simultaneously, without disturbing other students. It was originally described by Hoffman (1987) as part of his Oral Recitation Lesson, which is described in Chapter 6. Students select a passage of 50 to 100 words from their guided reading material. Then, in a soft and low voice, they spend five minutes practicing their passage. After the practice period, students read their passage aloud to the teacher, another student, or to the entire reading group.

Cooperative Repeated Reading

Cooperative repeated reading has been shown to improve students' reading fluency and general reading (Koskinen & Blum, 1984, 1986). In a 10- to 15-minute period during guided reading or independent reading, students work with a classmate or two on a short passage. Passages usually come from the basal text or trade book that is being used in guided reading. To do cooperative repeated reading, follow these steps:

1. Have partners find quiet, comfortable spots in the room for reading. Give each student a copy of the Cooperative Repeated Reading Response Form. (See Figure 4.6 on page 105.)
2. Have one student read his or her passage to a partner three times. Ask the partner to listen and provide assistance where necessary. The partner should also give feedback on the student's reading, based on the response sheet's criteria.
3. Have students reverse roles and repeat step 2.

A Center Approach to Repeated Reading Instruction

You may want to establish a repeated reading center that students go to at designated periods each day for 15 to 20 minutes. The center should contain a set of passages at various levels of difficulty, with recorded versions of each passage available, if possible. Assign each student a set of passages at his or her instructional level. (See Figure 4.1 on page 94 for guidelines on determining readability levels.) When students enter the repeated reading center, their job should be clear: to practice their assigned passages several times through until they believe they can read them independently and fluently. Students who need a bit of oral reading support may opt to listen to a passage on tape while reading it aloud.

From time to time, check on how your students are doing by having them read the passages to you. Of course, a volunteer aide would help immensely here. The aide could keep track of materials and assess students, noting progress on charts similar to that in Figure 4.4 on page 97.

Students read and listen to a passage several times until they can read it fluently on their own.

Cooperative Repeated Reading Response Form

Figure 4.6

Reader: _____ **Rater:** _____ **Date:** _____

How did you partner read? Rate him or her in each of the following areas for the first and last reading.

Decoding (*was able to read the words correctly*)

First Reading: Outstanding········1········2········3········Good········4········5········Fair

Final Reading: Outstanding········1········2········3········Good········4········5········Fair

Pacing (*was able to read at a good pace where appropriate*)

First Reading: Outstanding········1········2········3········Good········4········5········Fair

Final Reading: Outstanding········1········2········3········Good········4········5········Fair

Expression (*was able to read with good expression and in phrases—not word by word*)

First Reading: Outstanding········1········2········3········Good········4········5········Fair

Final Reading: Outstanding········1········2········3········Good········4········5········Fair

The school library can also be used as a repeated reading center of sorts. Students can choose books at their instructional level, with accompanying recordings, and practice reading the book while listening to the tape until they feel they can read it on their own. At that point, they can read the book to the librarian or teacher aide who is in charge of the program.

Repeated Reading of High-Frequency Words and Phrases

Recent studies on reading indicate that even a limited amount of word reading practice, whether in the form of flash cards (Nicholson, 1998; Tan & Nicholson, 1997), word banks (Bear, Invernizzi, Templeton, & Johnston, 1996), or word walls (Cunningham, 1995), can have a beneficial effect on students' word recognition skills. Such practice activities require students to read orally isolated words to the point where they recognize those words quickly and accurately. Often high-utility or high-frequency words are chosen for such activities because students need to be able to recognize them quickly.

One potential drawback to reading words in isolation is that it may reinforce the notion that reading is simply about identifying individual words. This could lead to word-by-word reading in some children, which is potentially a problem because the word is not necessarily the carrier of essential meaning. In fact, some scholars argue that the phrase is the key component in gaining meaning through written text (Schreiber, 1980, 1987, 1991; Schreiber & Read, 1980). And a considerable amount of research has demonstrated that helping students learn to read in phrases will improve their reading fluency and overall reading achievement (Rasinski, 1990, 1994).

Nevertheless, there is value in learning high-frequency words. Because practicing them in isolation too much could have negative effects, I suggest that, along with a *limited* amount of practice of high-frequency words in isolation, students do repeated reading of these words in the context of short sentences and phrases. Figure 4.7 on pages 107–111 provides three lists of short sentences and phrases. Embedded in the lists are Fry's 300 "instant words" (Fry, 1980; Fry & Rasinski, 2007). According to Fry, these words make up approximately two thirds of all the words students will encounter in their elementary school reading. The first list in the chart contains Fry's first 100 words, the second list contains his second 100, and the third list contains his third 100. As a general rule of thumb, I recommend that students learn a minimum of approximately 100–200 high-frequency words each year, so the 300 words in Fry's list should be mastered sometime during the primary grades.

Repeated reading of a few phrases per week not only gives students the practice they need to learn high-frequency words, but also gives them practice in reading phrases, which is key to developing fluency and general proficiency.

Teaching the phrases is easy. Simply list five to ten phrases on a chalkboard or chart and practice reading them chorally with your students several times a day—it only takes seconds. Read the phrases once or twice at the beginning and end of each day, and right before lunch. Additionally, practicing the high-frequency word phrases is also a fine home-reading activity. Practicing these phrases is something that parents can understand and do easily with their children. Parents and teachers can easily create simple games and activities that give students practice with these all-important words. Activities might include putting the phrases on flashcards or notecards for quick practice, using multiple copies of the phrases on notecards to play bingo or concentration (match), saying and sorting the phrases by the number of words in each phrase, and saying the phrases in silly voices.

Phrases and Short Sentences for Repeated Reading Practice

Figure 4.7

First 100 Words

These phrases contain the first 100 words from the Fry Instant Word List (1980), which represent 50 percent of all the words children encounter in elementary school reading.

The people	Look for some people.
Write it down.	I like him.
By the water	So there you are.
Who will make it?	Out of the water
You and I	A long time
What will they do?	We were here.
He called me.	Have you seen it?
We had their dog.	Could you go?

(Figure 4.7, continued)

What did they say?
When would you go?
No way
A number of people
One or two
How long are they?
More than the other
Come and get it.
How many words?
Part of the time
This is a good day.
Can you see?
Sit down.
Now and then
But not me
Go find her.
Not now
At your house
From my room
It's been a long time.
Will you be good?
Give them to me.
Then we will go.
Now is the time.
An angry cat
May I go first?
Write your name.
This is my cat.
That dog is big.
Get on the bus.
Two of us
Did you see it?
The first word

One more time
We like to write.
All day long
Into the water
It's about time.
The other people
Up in the air
She said to go.
Which way?
Each of us
He has it.
What are these?
If we were older
There was an old man.
It's no use.
It may fall down.
With his mom
See the water
As big as the first
But not for me
When will we go?
How did they get it?
From here to there
Number two
More people
Look up.
Go down.
All or some
Did you like it?
A long way to go
When did they go?
For some of your people

Second 100 Words

These phrases contain the second 100 words from the Fry Instant Word List (1980), which represent some of the most common words students encounter in their reading.

Over the river

My new place

Another great sound

Take a little.

Give it back.

Only a little

It's only me.

I know why.

Three years ago

Live and play.

I need help.

I work too much.

Any old time

Through the line

Right now

Mother means it.

Same time tomorrow

Tell the truth.

A little boy

The following day

We came home.

We want to go.

Show us around.

Form two lines.

A small house also

Another old picture

Write one sentence.

Set it up.

A good man

After the game

Most of the animals

Our best things

Just the same

My last name

That's very good.

Think before you act.

Mother says to go now.

Where are you?

Try your best.

Move over.

We found it here.

Study and learn.

Kind of nice

Spell your name.

The good American

Change your clothes.

Play it again.

Back off.

Give it away.

Answer the phone.

Turn the page.

The air is warm.

Read my letters.

It's still here.

Where in the world

We need more.

(Figure 4.7, continued)

Put it there.

Where does it end?

I don't feel well.

My home is large.

It turned out well.

Read the sentence.

This must be it.

Hand it over.

Such a big house

The men asked for help.

A different land

They went here.

Get to the point.

Because we should.

Even the animals

It's your place.

Good things

I study in school.

I'm an American.

Such a mess

Point it out.

Right now

It's a small world.

Big and small

Home sweet home

Around the clock

Show and tell.

You must be right.

Tell the truth.

Good and plenty

Help me out.

It turned out well.

I think so.

Read the book.

Third 100 Words

These phrases contain the third 100 words from the Fry Instant Word List (1980), which represent some of the most common words students encounter in their reading. The complete list of 300 words contains approximately two thirds of all the words students encounter in their reading.

Near the car

Between the lines

My own father

In the country

Add it up.

Read every story.

Below the water

Plants and flowers

Will it last?

Keep it up.

Stay a while.

A few good men

Don't open the door.

You might be right.

It seemed too good.

Along the way

Next time

It's hard to open.

Something good

For example

Plant the trees.
Light the fire.
The light in your eyes
In my head
Under the earth
We saw the food.
Close the door.
The big city
We started the fire.
It never happened.
A good thought
Do it often.
We walked four miles.
Until the end
A second later
Stop the music.
Read your book.
Sing your song.
State your case.
I miss you.
A very important person
On my side
I took the car.
So far so good.
The young girl
My feet hurt.
The dark night
A good idea
It began to grow.
Watch the river.
White clouds
Too soon
Leave it to me.
I hear the waves.
Almost enough

In the beginning
Those other people
A group of friends
We got together.
We left it here.
Both children
It's my life.
Always be kind.
Read the paper.
Run for miles.
Once upon a time
Is it really true?
It's time to eat.
Let me carry it.
Near the sea
Talk to my father.
The young face
The long list
My family
I cut myself.
Above the clouds
Watch the game.
The peaceful Indians
Without a care
I like being on the team.
The tall mountains
Next to me
A few children
A long life
A group of Indians
He started to cry.
I hear the sea.
An important idea
The first day of school
Almost four miles

➤ Concluding Thoughts

Repeated reading is a powerful tool. However, in many classrooms, repeated reading is rarely done. Teachers and students tend to read a selection once, talk about it a bit, and then move on to the next selection. But there is much to be gained from reading a text more than once. When repeated reading is employed on a regular basis and in engaging ways, students' word recognition, reading fluency, and comprehension improve significantly.

∾ Chapter 5 ∾

Performance Reading

Turning Research on Repeated Reading into Engaging and Effective Instruction

"The longer I live, the more I see there's something about reciting rhythmical words aloud—it's almost biological—that comforts and enlivens human beings."

—Robert Pinsky, Former U. S. Poet Laureate

Repeated reading is a powerful tool. Nevertheless, it is woefully underused in most elementary and middle-grade classrooms. In some cases, teachers are not fully aware of the benefits of repeated reading. In other cases, they may feel that reading a text more than once is an artificial task and, therefore, not worth asking of students. In still other classrooms, all the focus on improving students' reading speed in recent years has led to repeated reading becoming a quest to read faster and faster—a not terribly authentic use of reading.

Yet, as I pointed out in Chapter 4, repeated reading is beneficial for students who are significantly behind in their reading development. The improvements those students see in their reading performance can be highly motivating. But for more normally developing and advanced readers, repeated reading is often not very motivating or satisfying.

So while the science of teaching reading tells us that repeated reading can be an effective instructional strategy, the art of teaching reading challenges us to make repeated reading engaging for all students. Is it possible to make repeated reading an inherently interesting and engaging task for both students who are struggling as well as those who are developing at a normal or advanced rate?

The answer is yes—when we give students real reading tasks that demand practice, such as performance reading for an audience. Performance reading is a powerful instructional tool because it requires students to use repeated reading in preparation for their performances, and to read for meaning and understanding before and during their performances. It requires plenty of planning and practice time. But the end result—students who read with expression, fluency, and meaning—will show that this is time well spent.

There are several forms of performance reading. In this chapter, I describe several of the most effective and authentic types—student-led read aloud, readers' theater, poetry reading, and singing (remember, though, that many other forms of performance reading exist, such as jokes [Ness, 2009])—and I suggest ways to make them an integral and exciting part of any classroom experience.

➤ Student-Led Read Aloud

In Chapter 2, I describe teacher-led read aloud as a powerful oral reading strategy. Student-led read aloud can be equally powerful. When we read a text to students, we must practice beforehand to ensure that our reading is expressive, meaningful, and satisfying to the audience. The same is true for students who read aloud to others. Below are some ways to implement student-led read aloud.

Radio Reading

In radio reading, students read aloud a portion of a text assigned by you, sounding as much like a professional radio announcer as possible. As such, they must practice their reading at school and at home, by themselves and with partners, to perfect their performance. (For more information on radio reading, see Chapter 4.)

Book Talks

Some teachers designate times for students to read aloud to classmates, in whole-group and small-group contexts. Fifth-grade teacher Hannah Maxwell has her students give oral book reports, or "book talks." The goal of the book talk is not only for students to share their views on a book they've read recently, but also to "sell" the book to fellow students. Hannah asks her students to give a summary of the book, critique it, and read a favorite passage that illustrates a key event or illustrates the author's writing style. To make the book as exciting as possible, students need to read their passage with expression. And, for that to happen, they need to practice.

Book Buddies

Cross-age tutoring has been found to have significant advantages for both the tutor and the tutee. One way to implement cross-age tutoring is through pairing students at different grade levels to read aloud together as "book buddies." Book buddies meet periodically, usually once or twice a week, for 20 to 30 minutes before, during, or after school. The older student may read to the younger student, the younger student may read to the older student, or the two students may read aloud together. Whoever reads must practice beforehand so that his or her buddy reaps the full benefits of the experience, which is especially powerful for older struggling readers. Practicing on material that is at their younger buddy's level exposes these readers to the easier material they need to read to develop their own reading power. And rather than balking at being forced to read "baby" books, older readers see the activity as a chance to help and take responsibility for their buddy. For more advanced readers, the chance to read easier material from time to time builds fluency and expression. Younger readers also benefit from reading to a partner, especially if they have a chance to practice beforehand.

Recorded Books

If forming book buddies presents logistical difficulties, you can forge connections between older and younger students with tape-recorded books. In Chapter 3, I describe how recorded books can be a form of oral assisted reading in which students read a text and listen to a fluent rendition of it at the same time. Prerecorded books and other materials can be purchased from commercial sources, of course, but they can also be created by your students themselves. (See Chapter 3, page 85 for details.) Older students can record books for younger students. Usually, a difference of two grade levels is ideal—grade 5 students make recorded books for grade 3, grade 4 students for grade 2, and so forth.

Younger students appreciate reading text while they listen to the same materials read in an expressive voice by an older schoolmate, and the students who make the tapes benefit as well. To reach the level of fluency required to make a high-quality recording, the older students must practice reading the text several times through. As with book buddies, recorded books as a strategy is particularly beneficial for struggling older readers who need to read easier material to gain proficiency. Making books on tape for younger students gives them a good reason to read books that might otherwise embarrass them. It also provides a reason to do repeated reading.

Developing recorded books is not only a natural way to promote repeated reading, it is also motivating and potentially lucrative. Opitz and Rasinski (2008) tell the story of a class of intermediate-grade students who made recorded books for the primary grades. Students got so immersed in the project, they began selling their recorded tapes to parents to use with their children at home.

See a readers' theater in action on the DVD.

➤ Readers' Theater

Script reading is another form of performance reading that requires practice. However, when most teachers think of script reading, they think of putting on plays and all that goes with it: memorizing lines, learning movements, and creating costumes, props, and scenery—all of which requires a lot of time. And devoting time to staging plays takes time away from reading and other subject areas.

Fortunately, there is another type of script reading that is more manageable: readers' theater. In readers' theater, students stand in front of an audience, usually made up of their classmates, and read from scripts that they hold in their hands or are set on music stands. No costumes, props, or scenery are required unless the teacher and students wish to include them. Very little, if any, movement is involved. In a sense, readers' theater is a minimalist form of performing a play.

Without movement, costumes, props, or scenery, the performers have only one attribute to make their performance meaningful and satisfying: their voices. And, to use their voices well, performers must practice the text beforehand.

A Readers' Theater Snapshot

Six students stand in front of their classmates, about to perform "The Three Billy Goats Gruff." They wear no costumes, but have signs around their necks identifying the characters they are portraying. Three students are the goats, one is the mean old troll, and two share the role of the narrator. There are no scenery or props, except for six music stands holding copies of a script version of the beloved tale. The narrators stand off to one side. The three goats stand together in the middle of the "stage" with the troll only slightly away from them. The students read the script with as much expression and gusto as possible. When the troll is banished and the performance ends, the audience bursts into honest, appreciative applause.

Carrying Out Readers' Theater

Readers' theater is an authentic, entertaining, and educationally powerful way to read and communicate meaning. When implemented properly, it offers many opportunities for students to practice reading in multiple and meaningful ways. (See Figure 5.1 on pages 121–122 for guidelines on implementing readers' theater.) And we are gaining evidence from classroom research that readers' theater yields improvements in students' word recognition, fluency, and comprehension.

Martinez, Roser, and Strecker (1999), for example, implemented a readers' theater curriculum in two second-grade classrooms over a ten-week period. Claire Carter and Ed Meneses, the teachers in the study, divided their classes into three "repertory groups" of six to nine students. On Mondays, each repertory group was given a different script developed from trade books to learn for the week. The teachers read the books expressively to the class on the first day of the week and then gave a brief mini-lesson on some aspect of fluency, such as trying to read as if you were the character, adjusting reading pace, pausing at the end of sentences, reading with appropriate volume, or emphasizing individual words or phrases. Two copies of the scripts were then distributed to the repertory groups, one for practice at school and one for home.

The teachers devoted 30 minutes per day to readers' theater instruction. On Tuesdays through Thursdays, students practiced all parts of the scripts, received feedback, auditioned for parts, and were assigned roles. They discussed the meaning of their stories and issues related to staging the performance. They were also encouraged to practice the scripts at home. Over the course of the week, students read their scripts 15 to 20 times!

On Fridays, the groups read their scripts for a live audience made up of classmates, schoolmates, and parents, the school principal, and other school personnel. The class was motivated to perform for a real audience. Claire Carter noted, "The audience effect was important. The anticipation of an audience is what made reading practice seem like a dress rehearsal." Readers' theater turned repeated reading into an authentic and engaging experience for students.

The researchers measured students' reading performance prior to the project and at its conclusion ten weeks later. They also tracked the performance of two similar second-grade classrooms that received instruction with the same books, but without readers' theater. During the ten-week period, the readers' theater classrooms exhibited a fluency gain of 17 words per minute in reading

In readers' theater, students rely on their voices—and not costumes, props, or scenery—for a successful performance.

unrehearsed text. The comparison classrooms made less than half that gain in their fluency—fewer than seven words per minute.

The authors also administered informal reading inventories before starting and ten weeks later at the end of the readers' theater program to determine overall progress in reading, including comprehension. Among the 28 students in the readers' theater classrooms, 9 students made gains of two grade levels and 14 of one grade level. On average, students gained approximately 1.1 years during the ten-week study. Among the 28 students in the comparison classrooms, only 3 students made gains of two grade levels, 13 gained one grade level, and 12 showed no improvement in their reading performance at all. The average gain for student in the non-readers' theater groups was less than half of what was found in the readers' theater classrooms.

Some of the most compelling evidence came from the journals that students kept during the study. Omar wrote, "Readers' theater is the funnest reading I've ever did before!" Lucia wrote, "I never thought I could be a star, but I was the BEST reader today."

The teachers offered their own thoughts on the power of readers' theater. Claire Carter wrote about the pervasive power that the scripts and the practice of those scripts had on students' reading and writing: "They read those [original] books during their reading time. They wrote about the work and their own plays based on the same characters. They wrote story extensions of the scripts . . .

[They] repeatedly asked, 'Is it time for readers' theater?'" The authors concluded that readers' theater "promoted oral reading fluency, as children explored and interpreted the meaning of literature."

Second-grade teacher Chase Young (Young & Rasinski, 2009) made readers' theater an integral and daily part of his classroom literacy curriculum—devoting 5–20 minutes per day to fluency. Each week ended with Fluency Friday, during which students performed the materials they had been rehearsing all week. By the end of the year, students had made nearly twice the gain in fluency expected of normal-achieving second-grade students (Hasbrouck and Tindal, 2006) and were well above expectations in overall reading achievement.

Equally important for Chase was the motivational value of using readers' theater as a vehicle for fluency development: "As a classroom teacher, it was amazing to see the desire to entertain audiences with their prosodic reading. Because of their motivation to practice, refine, and perform texts, an academic avenue was created to increase reading fluency, read multiple text types, and include every student—striving or thriving. It was relatively easy to implement, fun, and instilled confidence in the young readers." Even the school secretary, who was a frequent guest for Fluency Fridays, noted that it was "absolutely wonderful to see students enjoying learning!"

Although readers' theater is often thought of as a primary-grade activity, Worthy and Broaddus (2001) remind us that it can be applied in the upper grades for developing fluency and promoting thoughtful, enjoyable engagements with texts.

After hearing of the success of the second-grade students in the Martinez, Roser, and Strecker study, fourth-grade teacher Lorraine Griffith decided to try it out during the better part of the 2000–2001 school year. She followed a format similar to the Martinez, Roser, and Strecker study: Monday—introduction of scripts and performance texts; Tuesday through Thursday—practice and rehearsal; Friday—performance. (See Figure 5.1 on pages 121–122 for details.) Lorraine was amazed at the results. Her five Title I students made average gains of three grade levels during the year, and her entire class passed the state-mandated proficiency examination in reading, which had not happened in previous years.

Lorraine attributes the success to readers' theater and the repeated reading that it requires. According to her, "The practice made them better readers and it also made them better writers." As students became familiar with the rich vocabulary and interesting sentences and phrases in the scripts, they began to try out the words and techniques in their own writing.

Lorraine has embedded repeated reading, readers' theater, and other forms of performance reading seamlessly into her fourth-grade literacy curriculum (Griffith & Rasinski, 2004). Three years of data have convinced her of the value of practice and performance. Struggling readers in Lorraine's classroom make, on average, 2.9 years growth in reading in the one year they are in her class. Normal fluency growth for fourth graders is about 29 words correct per minute. In Lorraine's classroom, the growth has been 59 words correct per minute!

Title I teacher Lisa Samuda knows the benefits of repeated reading but has struggled with implementing it in her own pull-out program, in which she sees small groups of students for 30 minutes per day, three to five times per week. She has developed her own innovative approach for using readers' theater. She finds out from the classroom teacher what her students have, are, or will be reading for guided reading instruction. Then, either on her own or with her students (if the students have already read the story in guided reading), Lisa develops the text, or a portion of the text, into a script and makes enough copies for her students to read with her during instruction time and at home. Over the course of the next several days, they practice their script. Then, when they feel they have mastered it, the students return to their classroom where they perform their script for their classmates. It is a real motivator for these students who are often viewed as the lowest performers to become the stars every week or two. According to Lisa, "I have kids who read well come up to me and ask how they can get into my Title I class!"

Figure 5.1

Readers' Theater: A Quick Guide

Before the Week Begins:
1. Select or write a script(s) to be performed. Make two copies (one for school, one for home) for each member of the repertory group.

Monday:
2. Introduce or review the nature, purpose, and procedures for readers' theater with the class.
3. Read (model) the script(s) to students while they follow along silently so that they can hear (and read) a fluent rendering of the script.

(Figure 5.1, continued)

4. Assign individual parts by having students volunteer or
   audition. Parts can also be assigned by students within groups
   and can rotate from one performance to another.

Tuesday:

5. Chorally read the script(s) as a class or in small groups (one
   to three times) so that you and your students can support one
   another in the reading.

Wednesday–Thursday:

6. Have students practice their parts on their own, in their
   group, under your guidance, and at home.

Friday:

7. Invite students to perform their scripts for an audience,
   usually their classmates, though others can be invited as well:
   schoolmates, parents, the principal. Try to make the performance a special event. Many teachers turn Friday afternoons
   into a "classroom readers' theater festival" at which many
   repertory groups perform their scripts.

Where to Find Scripts

"Where do you find the scripts to use with your students?" is a question that
often comes up when I talk to teachers about readers' theater. There are
many sources.

Published Collections

Check the school library for short scripts. In Figure 5.2 on pages 123–124, I
list some recent collections that should be on the shelf, along with commercial
publishers that specialize in scripts for elementary and middle-grade classrooms.
In my experience, these publishers produce quality scripts at a reasonable cost.

Look to instructional materials you already have. Many basal readers and
classroom newspapers contain scripts. There are also many Web sites devoted to

readers' theater that offer scripts at no cost. All you have to do is print them out and share them with students. Some of my favorites are also listed in Figure 5.2.

Regardless of the source, be sure to check the quality and length of scripts before you assign them. Those that exceed five pages (15 minutes to perform) will probably be too challenging for many students to read and too long to hold the attention of an audience of elementary students, especially if you are planning more than one reading per performance.

Readers' Theater Script Sources

Figure 5.2

Collections and Guides

Readers' Theater for Building Fluency: Strategies and Scripts for Making the Most of This Highly Effective, Motivating, and Research-Based Approach to Oral Reading by Jo Worthy (Scholastic, 2005)

Reader's Theatre for Beginning Readers by Suzanne Barchers (Teachers Ideas Press, 1993)

Presenting Readers' Theater by Caroline Feller Bauer (H. W. Wilson, 1991)

The Best of Readers' Theater, Vols. I and II, by Lisa Blau (One from the Heart, 2000)

A Reader's Theatre Treasury of Stories by Win Braun and Carl Braun (Braun & Braun, 2000)

Plays Around the Year, compiled by Liza Schafer and Mary Beth Spann (Scholastic, 1994) (grades 1–3)

25 Mini-Plays: World History by Erin Fry (Scholastic, 2000) (grades 4–8)

12 Fabulously Funny Fairy Tale Plays by Justine McCory Martin (Scholastic, 2002) (grades 2–4)

(Figure 5.2, continued)

Publishers of Readers' Theater Scripts

Teacher Created Materials (www.teachercreatedmaterials.com)
Search for "readers' theater," "practice and performance," and
"texts for fluency practice."
Reading A–Z (www.readinga-z.com/guided/theater_list.html)
Readers Theatre Script Service
(www.readerstheatreinstitute.com/scriptservice.html)
Benchmark Education Publishing
(www.benchmarkeducation.com) Search "readers' theater."

Web Sites

www.timrasinski.com
www.timelessteacherstuff.com
www.aaronshep.com/rt
www.readers-theatre.com
www.readinglady.com
www.teachingheart.net/readerstheater.htm
www.readerstheatre.ecsd.net/collection.htm
http://pbskids.org/zoom/activities/playhouse
www.literacyconnections.com/ReadersTheater.php
www.fictionteachers.com/classroomtheater/theater.html

Teacher-Created Scripts

You can also create scripts yourself, and trade books are a great source of inspiration. Many trade books are written in script form; students can read directly from the book during performances. But, in most cases, you'll need to adapt the text. Figure 5.3 on pages 125–126 provides a list of some of my favorite books that can be turned into scripts with little or no work on your part.

Think of the published material that you share with students in read aloud or guided reading—trade books, as well as poems and speeches. How might they be used or adapted for readers' theater? Stories with interesting characters, lively dialogue, and interesting problems work best. If you're considering a lengthy story or chapter book, think about adapting only a portion of it. Poetry, chants, cheers, and speeches can easily be broken into two or more parts, thus turning what might normally be considered a monologue into a form of readers' theater.

Figure 5.3

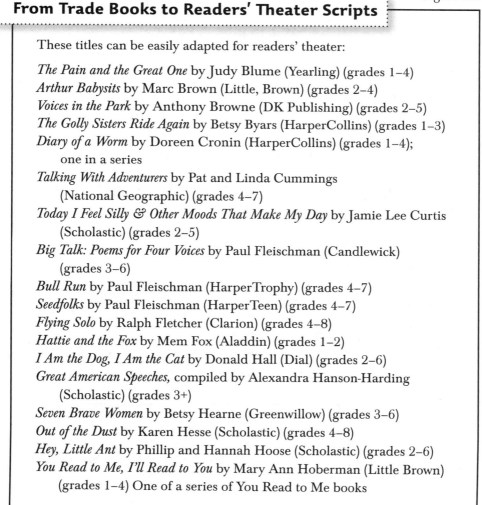

From Trade Books to Readers' Theater Scripts

These titles can be easily adapted for readers' theater:

The Pain and the Great One by Judy Blume (Yearling) (grades 1–4)
Arthur Babysits by Marc Brown (Little, Brown) (grades 2–4)
Voices in the Park by Anthony Browne (DK Publishing) (grades 2–5)
The Golly Sisters Ride Again by Betsy Byars (HarperCollins) (grades 1–3)
Diary of a Worm by Doreen Cronin (HarperCollins) (grades 1–4);
     one in a series
Talking With Adventurers by Pat and Linda Cummings
     (National Geographic) (grades 4–7)
Today I Feel Silly & Other Moods That Make My Day by Jamie Lee Curtis
     (Scholastic) (grades 2–5)
Big Talk: Poems for Four Voices by Paul Fleischman (Candlewick)
     (grades 3–6)
Bull Run by Paul Fleischman (HarperTrophy) (grades 4–7)
Seedfolks by Paul Fleischman (HarperTeen) (grades 4–7)
Flying Solo by Ralph Fletcher (Clarion) (grades 4–8)
Hattie and the Fox by Mem Fox (Aladdin) (grades 1–2)
I Am the Dog, I Am the Cat by Donald Hall (Dial) (grades 2–6)
Great American Speeches, compiled by Alexandra Hanson-Harding
     (Scholastic) (grades 3+)
Seven Brave Women by Betsy Hearne (Greenwillow) (grades 3–6)
Out of the Dust by Karen Hesse (Scholastic) (grades 4–8)
Hey, Little Ant by Phillip and Hannah Hoose (Scholastic) (grades 2–6)
You Read to Me, I'll Read to You by Mary Ann Hoberman (Little Brown)
     (grades 1–4) One of a series of You Read to Me books

(Figure 5.3, continued)

I Have a Dream by Martin Luther King Jr. (Scholastic) (grades 3–8)

Fables by Arnold Lobel (HarperTrophy) (grades 3–5)

Fox at School by Edward Marshall (Puffin) (grades 1–3); one in a series

Wings: A Tale of Two Chickens by James Marshall (Viking) (grades 2–4)

The Salamander Room by Anne Mazer (Knopf) (grades 2–4)

Cinder-Elly by Frances Minters (Viking) (grades 1–3)

King of the Playground by Phyllis Reynolds Naylor (Atheneum)
     (grades 2–4)

Once Upon a Cool Motorcycle Dude by Kevin O'Malley
     (Walker Books for Young Readers) (grades 3–7)

Pink and Say by Patricia Polacco (Philomel) (grades 3–8)

Easy-to-Read Folk and Fairy Tale Plays by Carol Pugliano (Scholastic)
     (grades 1–3)

Ring! Yo! by Chris Raschka (DK Publishing) (grades 1–3)

Yo! Yes? by Chris Raschka (Scholastic) (grades 1–3)

Dear Mrs. LaRue: Letters from Obedience School by Mark Teague
     (Scholastic) (grades 2–6); one in a series

The Teacher from the Black Lagoon by Mike Thaler (grades 2–5)
     One of the series of Black Lagoon books

Tell Me a Story, Mama by Angela Johnson (Orchard) (grades 1–3)

Mississippi Mud: Three Prairie Journals by Ann Turner (HarperCollins)
     (grades 2–6)

Rosie and Michael by Judith Viorst (Atheneum) (grades 2–4)

Morris the Moose by Bernard Wiseman (HarperTrophy) (grades 1–3);
     one in a series

The Horrible Holidays by Audrey Wood (Dial) (grades 2–4)

*I Was Dreaming to Come to America: Memories from the Ellis Island Oral
     History Project*, selected by Veronica Lawlor (Penguin) (grades 4–8)

Stephanie Wells, a fourth-grade teacher, converts many of her basal readers' stories into scripts, in her own handwriting, and makes copies for her students. It usually takes her about two hours per story from start to finish. She often gets creative, removing parts and characters when a story is too long and adding parts and dialogue if it needs a little "oomph." She also notes that her additions keep her students on their toes—they love to compare her adapted versions to the originals. Although adapting stories takes time, Stephanie says that once they are done, "You have them forever, or as long as you use that particular reading series." She sees it as time well spent.

I am an American history fan and have found that speeches from our nation's past are wonderful for readers' theater. Speeches, after all, are meant to be presented orally. Recall, however, when you had to memorize and recite a famous speech in school. If you are like most people, you found the assignment dreadful—memorizing and reciting a speech out of context is an inherently boring and potentially intimidating activity that doesn't give the reader or listener a sense of the events that inspired the speech. Readers' theater, however, offers an antidote. As a readers' theater script, the speech does not need to be memorized, just read with expression. Moreover, the script can be used as a springboard to discuss the reasons for which it was written—the events that led up to its original reading.

In the appendix, I include several of my own creations and adaptations for performance. The first is an adaptation of Sojourner Truth's famous speech, "Ain't I a Woman?" Parts for narrators and other performers are woven into the script, which describes events and the climate that inspired a significant part of American history and oratory. By reading the script orally, students (performers and audience members alike) understand why the speech was given and why it had such an impact on history. The Sojourner Truth speech is a great script to use during Black History Month, Women's History Month, or any other appropriate time of the year.

The second script is an adaptation of Clement Moore's famous poem, "The Night Before Christmas." Inspired by the work of Paul Fleischman (*Joyful Noise: Poems for Two Voices*) and Mary Ann Hoberman (You Read to Me, I'll Read to You series), I broke the classic poem into three parts: one part to be performed by one reader, another part to be performed by a second reader, and a third part to be performed by both readers chorally. This adaptation took only a matter of minutes and demonstrates how easy it is to adapt poems and other texts into a readers' theater format.

Student-Created Scripts

If we teachers can adapt texts for readers' theater, students should be able to do so as well. In fact, having students create their own scripts is a natural extension of readers' theater. It's a wonderful response activity after they have read or heard a story. (See Chapter 2.) For those who may disagree, who may think turning a story into a script is an inauthentic writing activity, remember that Hollywood is filled with scriptwriters who adapt novels for the screen every day—and get paid very well for doing it.

Many trade books can be transformed by students into readers' theater scripts. For example, in Ginger Thompson's sixth-grade classroom, pairs of students transformed (and later practiced and performed) *I Am the Dog, I Am the Cat* by Donald Hall into parodies entitled *I Am the Book, I Am the Computer; I Am a Democrat, I Am a Republican; I Am a Lizard, I Am a Frog*; and *I Am Deciduous, I Am Coniferous*.

When students turn stories into scripts, it is a variable scaffolded experience in writing. In other words, the original text acts as a model and a scaffold for student writers. To write their script, students must analyze deeply the well-formed writing of the author. They need to emulate the work of a good writer. This is a "variable" form of scaffolding because students can rely as heavily or lightly as they wish on the original story. Novice or struggling writers may not wish to deviate much from the original text. They may retain most of the original text, but just turn it into script form. For example, Karen Alvarez, a third-grade teacher, likes to use Arnold Lobel's *Fables* when she introduces script writing to her students. "The stories are only one page long. They have lots of dialogue and very clear plots, with an explanatory moral at the end of each one. My struggling readers and writers do not even have to rewrite the text into script. With highlighters they can identify the parts to be read by the different characters. It is a super book to introduce students to writing scripts. Later on, my students transform those highlighted copies into more conventional scripts."

More advanced or ambitious writers often take more liberties, adding, changing, and deleting characters, dialogue, and scenes. Regardless of how close to or how far from the original text students stay or stray, the original text acts as a scaffold that supports their writing—a scaffold that students can go back to again and again for ideas, inspirations, and models.

Students love performing poems, scripts, and other texts that lend themselves to oral interpretation.

In the appendix, I have also included an adaptation of "The Three Billy Goats Gruff" that I did with second-grade students in the Kent State University Reading Clinic. Although students at the time had been doing readers' theater scripts, they were performing scripts created by others. They wanted to do one of their own, so we transformed a familiar folktale into a script that they eventually practiced and performed (to rave reviews). In writing the script, the students felt the goats were a bit too meek, so they took some creative liberty to give the goats some attitude by having the first two goats talk back to the troll when he allowed them to cross the bridge.

Weaving Readers' Theater Into Science

Readers' theater can be used in any content area. For example, Ken Beuther, a middle-school science teacher who recently earned his credentials in reading, has found ways to incorporate readers' theater into science. Periodically, he creates scripts that summarize and extend concepts he has covered recently with his students. One script that stands out is "The Adventures of Cell Boy," a fictional account of intrabody heroes at the cellular level who save weeds and flowers and, in the process, learn a bit about plant biology.

Tom Elkin, a fifth-grade teacher, uses readers' theater across his curriculum. He recently showed me a script his students had created about the planets and the solar system. The sun and the planets were the main characters. According to Tom, students performed the script several times and loved each presentation.

➤Reading and Performing Poetry

Poems, like scripts and speeches, are meant to be read aloud. Meaning is carried in a poem's oral interpretation, as well as in its words. And reading poetry has many benefits. The rhyme, rhythm, and repetition that pervade poetry—the elements that make reading it easy and fun—also serve to build fluency (Perfect, 1999, 2005; Faver, 2008; Rasinski, Rupley, & Nichols, 2008). Most children have had experience with poetry even before entering school, so they are familiar with its characteristics. Moreover, the brevity of most poems makes them especially appropriate for multiple readings.

Kathy Perfect (1999), a fourth-grade teacher, notes that the best way to teach poetry is to live it and experience it daily in the classroom:

> *"I strongly believe in immersing children daily in poetry of all kinds—rhymed and free verse, serious or silly—to help make poetic language both familiar and provocative. In my classroom, poetry begins our day, but it is never routine. Some days, on goes a mouse finger puppet that scoots across the top and down the sides of the book as I read poems from* Mice Are Nice *(Larrick, 1990). Other times, I might have one of the children put a hand puppet on while I read. But most of time, it's just me, the poetry, and my class. I allow the reading of it to pull us in."*

Each day, Kathy allots time to share poems that connect to the time of year, current events, areas of study, or the general mood of the class. Students are invited to share their favorite poems at this time—poems they've practiced. Impromptu poetry breaks happen often, too, during which Kathy and students may share a just-discovered poem. Group performances are also a regular feature of her reading program.

Poetry Coffeehouses

Several of my teacher acquaintances in primary through the middle grades catapult their classrooms back to the 1950s and 1960s when poetry performances were held in coffeehouses. (Today, these performances go by another name: "poetry slams.") Every Friday afternoon during the last hour or so of the day, they stage a "poetry coffeehouse" or "poetry party." Students prepare by spending some time on Monday morning listening to their teachers read poems, browsing through the poetry collections in the room, and selecting one or more poems to learn. At the coffeehouse, most poems are read by individual students, but some are read by pairs, trios, and larger groups. And there are always one or two poems that the whole class reads in choral style.

Students practice their selected poems throughout the week—in school, during recess, after school, and at home. The teacher usually provides time for listening to and coaching students in their readings. When Friday afternoon arrives, lights are lowered, shades are drawn, and table lamps are lit to create just the right mood. A barstool sits in the middle of the classroom "stage." A volunteer parent arrives with refreshments and the festivities begin.

The teacher (aka, the master of ceremonies) calls the coffeehouse to order. She begins with her own selection and introduces the performers for the day. Students, many dressed all in black and wearing beads and berets, come up one by one and read their selections, with the understanding that the key to a successful performance lies not only in the poet's words but also in their own interpretation of those words. Grand performances are rewarded with the snapping and clicking of fingers. Between sets, students often talk about the performances. In one classroom, bongos and tambourines mysteriously appeared to provide musical interludes between and accompaniment to the readings.

Visitors are always welcome at these poetry coffeehouses. The school principal, parents, and other teachers often show up. The cost of admission is a poem to share with the audience, of course. After all the poems have been recited—individually, in pairs, in small groups and large—and the refreshments consumed, the day ends, and students, fortified with the power and voice of poetry, go home chanting, "Carpe diem!"

I'm continually amazed at the seriousness with which students treat the poetry coffeehouses. One of my most vivid memories involves a struggling fourth grader who, one cold afternoon in January with the wind blowing and snow falling, read his father's favorite poem, "The Cremation of Sam McGee" by Robert Service, a poem about the unusual characters inhabiting the frigid Canadian Yukon during the Gold Rush. This youngster awed his classmates by reading with amazing conviction and expression. He received the loudest applause (and finger snapping) of the day. This student, who had not met with much success as a reader before, learned how reading has the power to transform. This one performance led the class to examine the body of work by Service. Several weeks later, the entire coffeehouse was devoted to the "rough and tough" poems of Robert Service.

After observing these classroom coffeehouses over several years, I have noticed an interesting pattern. In September, students are most likely to choose silly poems by the likes of Shel Silverstein and Jack Prelutsky. By mid-year, teachers guide students to more serious and thoughtful poetry. (For example, during the recent centennial of Langston Hughes' birth, one classroom of fourth graders spent January studying, reading, and performing the poetry of the Harlem Renaissance.) Toward the end of the year, students eagerly write their own poetry, often modeled after the poems and poets they had been performing previously, so the coffeehouses begin to feature a combination of published and original work. This is a very exciting evolution to witness.

Interestingly, most of these teachers deny teaching poetry in the traditional way. Instead, they use poetry as a vehicle for studying the richness of language and human creativity. And they and their students use poetry coffeehouses as a vehicle for celebrating what they learn. The fact that students grow to love poetry and write their own is a natural outcome of this immersion.

For those few of you who may be saying to yourself, "I just don't like poetry, I'm not sure that I can get my students to like it," I think there are reasons for your dislike that require some analysis. The first reason is that in high school you probably had to read a poem silently and then were required to analyze it and discover the poet's interpretation. That sort of response is likely to kill anyone's interest in poetry. In our reading program, we do not make students analyze poems. We may ask them to talk about why they chose a poem and what they think it means to them personally, but we do not go further. A poem means whatever a reader may want it to mean. Sometimes the meaning is universal; often, it is deeply personal.

The second reason why people may not like poetry comes from the notion of repeated reading itself. A poem is like a song—it has to be experienced repeatedly.

Have you ever heard a song on the radio on a Monday morning for the first time and not liked it? However, if you listen to it repeatedly all week long, by Friday it may be your favorite song of all time! Like a song, a poem has to be experienced repeatedly. It is only after hearing or reading a poem several times through that I begin to notice the rhythm, rhyme, alliteration, assonance, voice, imagery, metaphor, or other devices that the poet has used in his or her creation. Poems are meant to be read repeatedly—that is when enjoyment and appreciation happen or are deepened.

Can't-Miss Poets for Children and Adolescents

Classics

Hilaire Belloc	Henry Wadsworth Longfellow
N. M. Bodecker	Ogden Nash
Lewis Carroll	James Whitcomb Riley
Samuel Taylor Coleridge	Christina Rossetti
Emily Dickinson	Carl Sandburg
Paul Laurence Dunbar	Robert Service
T. S. Elliot	Robert Louis Stevenson
Robert Frost	William Makepeace Thackeray
Langston Hughes	Ernest L. Thayer
Emma Lazarus	Walt Whitman
Edward Lear	

Contemporary

Arnold Adoff	Aileen Fisher
Maya Angelou	Douglas Florian
Brod Bagert	Kristine O'Connell George
John Ciardi	Nikki Giovanni
Joanna Cole	Eloise Greenfield
Kalli Dakos	Nikki Grimes
Barbara Juster Esbensen	David Harrison

Contemporary, continued

Georgia Heard	Myra Cohn Livingston
Aileen Fisher	David McCord
Paul Fleischman	Eve Merriam
Mary Ann Hoberman	Lillian Moore
Sara Holbrook	Kenn Nesbitt
Lee Bennett Hopkins	Jack Prelutsky
Paul Janeczko	Joyce Carol Thomas
Alan Katz	Shel Silverstein
X. J. Kennedy	Judith Viorst
Karla Kuskin	Carol Boston Weatherford
Bruce Lansky	Valerie Worth
Dennis Lee	Jane Yolen
J. Patrick Lewis	Charlotte Zolotow

➤ Songs and Song Lyrics

To a large extent, songs and song lyrics are like poems. They contain many of the same elements of poetry—they are pattern texts that contain rhyme and rhythm. And, like poems, songs are meant to read (sung) aloud and repeatedly. (Have you ever gotten up and heard a song in the morning and found yourself singing it to yourself aloud all day long? Songs are a natural for repeated readings!) Songs also manifest one other significant contextual element that is peculiar to songs and music—melody. Melody makes songs easier to master and remember. Moreover, melody may also be thought of as a form of prosody, an important element of fluency. For these reasons, the use of songs and singing in the classroom is ideal for teaching reading fluency.

The key to using songs for reading fluency is to ensure that students are actually tracking the written text visually, even when they have memorized the song lyrics. The rhythm, rhyme, and melody make songs easy to learn, easy to memorize. If students sing songs from memory without visually tracking the words in print, they are not really reading because reading requires the reader to keep his or her eyes on the words in print. So, when singing songs, be sure to remind students to keep tracking the words visually, even if they have the words memorized. (I sometimes will insert a misspelled word or two into the printed lyrics and ask students to see if they can find the misspelled word(s) as they read/sing the song.)

Songs allow us to connect with our culture. Think of all the songs that are drawn from American and world history. Here in the United States, we have songs from the American Revolution to the Civil War to the Civil Rights era and beyond (those of you who were in college in the 1960s and '70s will surely remember the song performed by Crosby, Stills, Nash, and Young about my university—"Four Dead in Ohio"). We have songs that come from every culture and that identify different times of the year. Songs can bring us together as a nation or a classroom community. And, of course, songs can inspire us, make us think, make us cry, and make us laugh.

Think about teaching students a new song every week, using much the same routine that you would for scripts, poems, and other texts. Model singing a song early in the instructional cycle for students who follow along, then sing it chorally and repeatedly, and eventually have students perform it on their own. In doing so, students will become better readers, and they may also experience the school curriculum in different ways.

Marissa Schum is a fifth-grade reading and social studies teacher. During the year, her students study the American Civil War. In addition to reading textbooks and trade books about this watershed moment in American history, she also has her students learn songs from the Civil War. Marissa says, "We have learned and sung 'The Battle Hymn of the Republic,' 'The Battle Cry of Freedom,' 'When Johnny Comes Marching Home Again,' and 'Goober Peas,' among others. When we sing and talk about the content of these songs, I see my students more engaged than ever. They see a side of American history that they cannot get from reading a book. It becomes a bit emotional for many of them. And, to top it off, I see them improving in reading as we read, sing, and read again these songs, choose words from the songs for deeper analysis and placement on the word wall, and talk about the deeper meanings that underlie the lyrics themselves." Indeed, Marissa is right on with her observations. Research is beginning to show that the repeated reading (singing) of song lyrics can have a dramatic impact on students' reading growth (Biggs, Homan, Dedrick, Minick, & Rasinski, 2008).

➤Concluding Thoughts

Performance reading has another benefit—one related to classroom management. Teachers who practice small-group instruction often express concern about the students with whom they're not working during small-group time. Are those students fully engaged in academic work, or are they doing simple-minded worksheets or chatting with friends? This is a real concern because, in many classrooms, a good amount of the school day is devoted to independent work. Performance reading—whether it's student-led read aloud, readers' theater, poetry reading, singing, or some other form of performance—offers at least one productive activity that students can engage in when the teacher is working with a group: practicing their texts. I've found that students appreciate this time for rehearsal and use it productively. In fact, in the classrooms I visit, teachers do not allot much direct instruction time to practice. Once a routine has been established, students are expected to rehearse at home or during free time in school. And independent practice in reading is a very productive use of their time.

Oral practice, or repeated reading, comes in many forms. It can be taught directly in all kinds of ways, as described in Chapter 4. Or it can be made a part of other, more collaborative oral reading activities, such as student-led read aloud, readers' theater, poetry reading, or singing. Regardless of how you use it, repeated reading can lead to improved word recognition, fluency, comprehension, and overall reading performance. I have been told that Hollywood and Broadway are filled with actors who experienced difficulty in reading while in school. I can't help but wonder if many of them intuitively discovered that the rehearsal involved in preparing for a performance of a play, television program, or motion picture helped them to overcome their reading difficulties (and also to build their confidence by basking in the public adulation that comes from being a star).

You now have a number of approaches for making repeated reading an important part of your curriculum. In the next two chapters, I explore how oral reading, including repeated reading, can be integrated successfully into the school day.

 **Chapter 6** 〜

Creating Synergy

Lessons That Integrate Oral Reading Activities to Create Even More Powerful Instruction

"I was encouraged to read aloud in class and vocalize."

—Bob Edwards, Radio Host and Personality (October 2000)

Joan Segrin, a Title I teacher, is a true believer in the importance of reading fluency. She has helped many students overcome reading difficulties by employing many of the instructional activities in this book—especially paired reading and repeated reading. When she implements one of these strategies, her students' progress is solid and steady. But when she combines strategies, the impact is even greater. "When my students do repeated reading in a paired reading format, they have even better gains than if they were to do those activities separately." Joan has discovered the notion of instructional synergy: combining strategies in ways that lead to powerful results, more powerful than if she implemented those strategies individually. For Joan, the whole of the instructional routine is definitely worth more than the sum of its parts.

In Chapters 2 through 5, I offered a variety of methods for using oral reading to teach literacy, from teacher-led read aloud to student-led performance reading. For each of these methods, I suggested a variety of engaging activities that have been found to build word recognition, reading fluency, comprehension, and overall reading. In this chapter, I introduce the notion of synergy—the logical combination of related activities with the same purpose—as it applies to oral reading instruction. Combining powerful elements of fluency instruction into an instructional routine delivered to students on a regular basis will result in instruction that is more effective than if the elements were presented separately. As you read this chapter, consider how these ideas might fit into your classroom and, more important, how you might devise your own forms of instructional routines that create synergy.

Teaching Tip: Combine Oral Reading Activities Daily

Imagine devising an extended lesson that combines teacher-led read aloud, oral support reading, and repeated reading, which you schedule for 60 minutes on Monday, Wednesday, and Friday. You are likely to get better results than if you spent 60 minutes doing read aloud on Monday, 60 minutes in oral support reading on Wednesday, and 60 minutes of repeated reading on Friday. Daily interaction of modeled, supported, and repeated reading produces better results than if you taught each activity separately.

▶Repeated Reading While Listening

In Chapter 3, I suggested using oral assisted reading (OAR) for building reading fluency. OAR activities require students to read a text while simultaneously listening to a fluent rendition of the same text—from a parent, teacher, or other more proficient reader, or from a recording. Reading a text while listening to it being read appears to reinforce recognition of words and phrases, which leads to improved reading. In Chapter 4, I discussed repeated reading—reading a text more than once to improve fluency, word recognition, and comprehension. One simple way to introduce synergy is to combine these two proven approaches. Research has shown that having students engage in repeated reading while simultaneously receiving the support of a fluent rendition results in improved reading performance, especially for struggling readers (Hasbrouck, Ihnot, & Rogers, 1999; Rasinski, 1990; Rasinski & Hoffman, 2003; Rasinski, Reutzel, Chard, & Linan-Thompson, in press; Smith & Elley, 1997). In the study reported by Smith and Elley, for example, during a daily 20- to 25-minute intervention, students repeatedly read and listened to high-interest stories on tape at their instructional levels until they felt they could read the stories on their own. Over 27 weeks (about three quarters of a normal school year), students made, on average, gains of 2.2 years in their reading achievement. Moreover, students who participated in this synergistic program maintained their progress in reading over a two-month summer break.

To do repeated reading while listening, set aside time daily for the student to read and reread passages at his or her instructional level, multiple times. The student reads while listening to a fluent rendition of the text, either by a person or on a recording. When the student feels he or she has achieved an appropriate level of fluency, check his or her reading by having the student read the passage aloud independently. Record the reading rate (words read correctly per minute) and accuracy scores (percentage of words read correctly) on a log sheet. From there, move the student on to another text that is at the same difficulty level or slightly more challenging than the previous one, depending on his or her performance.

▶Oral Recitation Lesson see p. 142-143

After studying the role of oral reading in traditional reading instruction since the 1800s, as well as scholarly literature on the impact of oral reading on struggling readers, James Hoffman (1987; Hoffman & Crone, 1985) developed the oral recitation lesson (ORL), an instructional procedure involving modeling, support and coaching, repeated reading, and performance. Easily implemented in a regular classroom where basal stories and informational passages are part of the reading program, ORL is particularly effective with low-achieving readers.

The lesson is made up of two basic components, direct instruction and indirect instruction, each containing several steps. (See Figure 6.3 on pages 142–144 for guidelines.)

The direct instruction component begins with the teacher reading a story to a group of several students. After the reading, the teacher and students engage in a discussion of the text and, on a chart or chalkboard, create a story map together that includes the story's basic elements. (See Figures 6.1 and 6.2.) The teacher scribes the students' responses verbatim, as in a language experience activity. The completed story map is used as a visual aid to construct a written summary of the story.

Figure 6.1

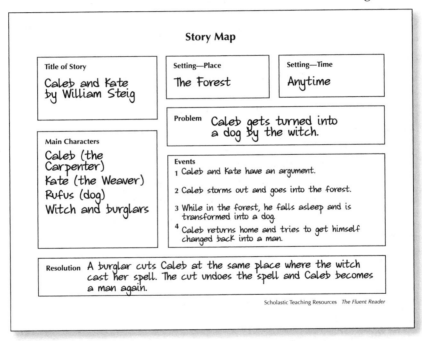

Story Map

Title of Story Caleb and Kate by William Steig	**Setting—Place** The Forest	**Setting—Time** Anytime

Problem Caleb gets turned into a dog by the witch.

Main Characters
Caleb (the Carpenter)
Kate (the Weaver)
Rufus (dog)
Witch and burglars

Events
1 Caleb and Kate have an argument.
2 Caleb storms out and goes into the forest.
3 While in the forest, he falls asleep and is transformed into a dog.
4 Caleb returns home and tries to get himself changed back into a man.

Resolution A burglar cuts Caleb at the same place where the witch cast her spell. The cut undoes the spell and Caleb becomes a man again.

Scholastic Teaching Resources *The Fluent Reader*

A completed story map

Hoffman describes the second part in the direct instruction component as fast-paced and interactive. In Jean Larson's class, this step begins with a mini-lesson on the importance of effective oral expression, focusing on aspects such as pitch, stress, and juncture. Then, with appropriate enthusiasm and expression, Jean reads a short section of the story upon which the map was based. Students then practice reading the segment, individually and/or chorally, with Jean

Story Map

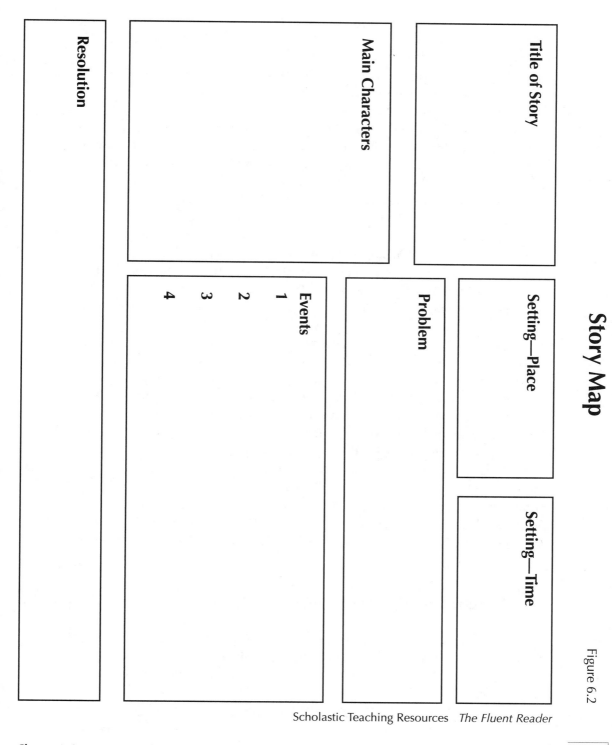

Title of Story

Main Characters

Setting—Place

Setting—Time

Problem

Events

1

2

3

4

Resolution

Scholastic Teaching Resources   *The Fluent Reader*

Figure 6.2

listening in and providing support and feedback to improve oral expression. Over time, as her students become more fluent in their reading, Jean reads longer sections of an entire page or more.

For the third part of the direct instruction component, Jean has her students select a passage from a text, usually about a page long, that they wish to perform. The students practice independently and then perform for the group. After each performance, Jean showers her students with useful comments, such as "Wow! You had great volume. We could all hear you well!" or "The expression you used helped me understand what the author was trying to say. Great job!"

The direct instruction component may require two to four reading-group sessions to complete. When the work on one story is complete, focus instruction on another story that is as or slightly more challenging than the one just read.

The indirect instruction component is a whole-class activity that takes approximately ten minutes. Students work with stories that were assigned earlier, in the direct instruction component. They practice reading their assigned story in a "soft," barely audible voice (also known as "mumble reading," described on page 103) so that all students can practice without disturbing one another. During this time, Jean works with individual students, checking for mastery. (Mastery for the second grade, according to Hoffman, is a minimum of 98 percent word recognition accuracy and 75-words-per-minute fluency, with good expression.) Once Jean signs a student off on one story, she moves him or her on to the next story that is as or slightly more challenging than the one just covered.

Hoffman (1987) reported that second-grade students using ORL made progress in reading, especially those who had made little progress previously. Students progressed from simple word identification to comprehension. Other research (Reutzel & Hollingsworth, 1993; Reutzel, Hollingsworth, & Eldredge, 1994) has found that students who received ORL made gains in both reading fluency and comprehension.

Figure 6.3

Oral Recitation Lesson: A Quick Guide

ORL is meant to be used in regular classroom settings, particularly with students experiencing difficulty in reading. Authentic narrative and informational passages from basal readers or trade books may be used.

Direct Instruction Component

(2 to 4 days per story, 30 to 45 minutes per day, done in small groups)

Part 1

1. Read the story aloud to students.
2. After the reading, work with students to construct a story map that contains major elements, including setting (time and place), characters, problem, and resolution to the problem. Act as a scribe and write the students' responses verbatim on a chart, whiteboard, or chalkboard.
3. Using the story map as a guide, write a brief, accurate, and complete story summary.
4. Select a memorable portion of the story (from a few sentences to an entire page or more) for the next step in the lesson.

Part 2

5. Provide a mini-lesson on the elements of good, expressive, and meaningful reading. Model a fluent oral reading of the memorable portion of the story that you selected.
6. Have students practice reading the selected portion alone, in pairs, and/or chorally. Coach them by giving feedback, support, and praise.

Part 3

7. Have students select a portion of the text for performance. Give them plenty of opportunities for practice and, when they're ready, have them perform the texts for their classmates. Be sure to offer positive feedback after every performance.

Indirect Instruction Component

(daily for approximately 10 minutes, done by the entire class)

1. Assign or ask students to choose a story, or a portion of a story, that has been covered in the direct instruction component.
2. Have students practice their story by mumble reading— reading in a soft, barely audible voice—so that all students can practice without disturbing one another.

(Figure 6.3, continued)

3. As they practice, check to see if students have achieved mastery in word recognition (98 percent word recognition accuracy) and fluency (75 words per minute, with good expression).
4. Assign the next story or passage to students who achieve mastery and repeat the process.

➤Fluency Oriented Reading Instruction

In a good example of how teachers adapt programs to work for their own instructional needs, Steven Stahl, Melanie Kuhn, and colleagues (Kuhn et al., 2006; Stahl & Heubach, 2005) modified Hoffman's oral recitation lesson to work specifically with basal reading programs and called it fluency oriented reading instruction (FORI).

FORI is a weekly, scaffolded instructional routine. In its intensive form, it begins with the teacher reading a story selection aloud to the class, while students follow along silently in their books. This is followed by a discussion of the story, including vocabulary, comprehension, and other instructional activities related to the story.

On the second day of instruction, the teacher echo-reads the story with students. He or she reads two or three sentences and then students orally read the same sentences. Again, the reading is followed by an instructional activity related to the text, such as writing a response. Students reread the same story aloud at home to or with a family member (this home reading can occur over several days). More fluent readers may be given an alternative assignment at home.

On the third day of instruction, students reread the story chorally with the teacher. He or she monitors students to ensure that they are actively engaged in reading. The fourth day involves partner reading—students reading orally with a partner, alternating pages. When not reading orally, the partner listens to and monitors his or her partner's reading. If time permits, partners can read the passage a second time, switching the pages that each partner reads. On the final day of the FORI routine, students complete extension activities related to the text. Over the course of the week, students read the assigned text at least four times, usually more.

Two fairly large-scale studies employing the FORI routine, as well as a modified version of FORI with second-grade students, found that students who received the fluency intervention made significantly greater gains in word recognition, comprehension, and overall reading achievement than students from the same schools who were given more traditional instruction from the existing instructional programs (Kuhn et al., 2006; Stahl & Heubach, 2005). In the Stahl and Heubach study, students made nearly two years of progress in one year of instruction. Moreover, at the end of the intervention, only 2 of 105 students were reading below grade level. Interestingly, Stahl and Heubach also reported that students made the greatest progress when the materials they were asked to read were somewhat challenging (at their frustration levels). Perhaps the scaffolded and repeated nature of the instructional fluency routine allowed students to handle more challenging texts, and, in doing so, they were able to accelerate their progress in reading.

►Fluency Development Lesson

Several years ago, my colleague Nancy Padak and I (Rasinski & Padak, 1998) examined the reading behavior of elementary students who were recommended by their classroom teachers to receive Title I instruction. We looked at various aspects of their reading, including decoding, fluency, and comprehension. Students in every grade, on average, performed below grade-level expectations in all three areas. However, one finding surprised us: The area in which students performed the lowest, by far, was reading fluency. Students read the connected text we gave them in such a slow, disjointed, and labored manner that we wondered how they could possibly understand any of it. We surmised that reading fluency is key to reading proficiency and that lack of fluency is a significant contributor to children's reading difficulties. Our conclusion was later confirmed in the findings of the National Reading Panel as well as in the reports of other researchers (e.g., Duke, Pressley, & Hilden, 2004).

In response to the findings of this study, we developed a synergistic lesson for teaching reading fluency called the fluency development lesson (Rasinski & Padak, 2008), which is outlined in Figure 6.4 on pages 148–149. As opposed to the weekly nature of FORI, the FDL is a daily scaffolded instructional routine.

FDL begins with the teacher reading aloud several times (modeling/repeated reading) a short, usually predictable text, such as a poem or a short passage from a basal story. Harry Parker, for example, uses his booming voice to draw his second graders into the daily poems that he uses in his fluency development lessons. Then, he repeats the poem in a variety of other voices, including a staccato, unexpressive, robot-like voice to illustrate disfluent reading, which his students dislike. Harry then spends a minute or two talking with his students about the meaning of the poem, as well as any difficult or unusual words.

Next, Harry and his students read the poem chorally several times, in various ways (oral support reading). He then pairs his students up, and each student reads the poem to his or her partner three times (repeated reading). The partner listens, provides help when necessary, and encourages the reader. Harry feels it is important to encourage the listeners to be supportive and give good feedback. After the third reading, the students reverse roles, and the listener becomes the reader.

After this practice time, Harry calls students together and offers them the opportunity to perform for an audience. The audience is usually the class itself, but sometimes Harry sends students off to perform for other classes; for the school principal, secretary, and janitor; for parent volunteers; or for teachers who aren't on duty (more repeated reading).

After the performances, Harry and his students choose two or three interesting words from the text and add them to their individual word banks and the classroom word wall. Later, these words are used for word practice, sorts, games, and other activities.

Harry extends FDL by making two copies of the poem for each student. The students keep one copy in their poetry folders so they can reread and enjoy it later. The other copy goes home. Each day, as homework, students must find as many people as possible to listen to them read their FDL poem (more repeated reading). Parents, grandparents, brothers, sisters, relatives, and neighbors listen to the student read his or her poem once, twice, or more. Harry prepares parents for this early in the school year. He not only tells them that their children will be reading a poem each day to develop fluency, but he also talks about the importance of repeated reading and encouragement. After each reading, the listener signs the back of the poem or the daily Lucky Listeners form (see Figure 6.5 on page 154) and adds a word or two of praise. This automatically enrolls the student in the "Lucky Listeners Club!" This activity has evolved into a friendly competition of who can come to class each morning with the greatest number of signatures. This is not only fun for the students, but it also tells Harry who's doing the most repeated readings. Harry and his students usually read the poem a couple more times chorally before moving on to the new poem for the day.

FDL is fast paced. Harry's entire lesson, for example, takes less than 15 minutes to complete. Once students get the hang of the routine, it doesn't need to be explained. So instead of listening to directions, Harry's students are reading—and they read a lot. Moreover, for students still struggling with fluency, this blend of modeled and supported reading is just what they need to be doing.

My research colleagues and I worked with second-grade teachers in urban schools, implementing FDL from May to October (Rasinski, Padak, Linek, & Sturtevant, 1994). We found that students made substantial gains in their reading fluency, as well as in their overall reading, as measured by an informal reading inventory. Indeed, their gains were greater than those of a similar group of students who spent the same amount of time with the same texts, but engaged in other forms of reading instruction. Moreover, we found that students and teachers enjoyed this lesson. Students became successful at reading FDL texts—and that success transferred to other, unfamiliar texts. Other research has supported the use of FDL with first-grade students (Kulich, Evanchan, & Sidorova, in press). Teacher and researcher Lynne Kulich has found the fluency development lesson to be perfect for her emerging readers:

> *While teaching first-, second-, and third-grade students, I implemented the FDL with poetry on a daily basis in my classroom. Each year, my classroom culture was enriched by the diversity of my students. Not only were monolingual English learners developing fluency and comprehension skills with the incorporation of the FDL, but my ELLs were also demonstrating great reading progress. Perhaps the most compelling reason for implementing the FDL is the level of student engagement evident in the classroom. The sheer desire to read for both aesthetic and efferent purposes began to escalate as the school year progressed. No other reading activity had such a powerful impact upon my diverse emergent readers.*

Perhaps the greatest evidence of FDL's effectiveness lies in its staying power. Teachers continued to practice it several years after the completion of the study. And we can see why: We have used a version of FDL in our university reading clinic for years and have found it to work consistently well with students of all ages who have difficulty with reading fluency.

Second-grade teacher Gail Evanchan, a long-time user of FDL, has customized it for her own classroom and style of teaching. In fact, she has authored her own poetry to be used in the lesson. "I have been using FDL in my classroom for four years now and have found it to be very successful. I have seen my students make great progress in their reading fluency. I realize it can be done using any passage, but I chose to use poetry. I usually do it first thing in the morning. The lessons take approximately 15 minutes. I have written enough poems to last the entire school year on large chart paper and try to correlate the poems with curricular themes or seasonal activities."

Figure 6.4

Fluency Development Lesson: A Quick Guide

Do FDL on a regular basis, daily if possible. Use short passages of about 100 to 200 words; highly predictable poems work well, as do consecutive segments of a short story read over several days. Make two copies of the FDL text for each student. Put the text on chart paper for choral reading.

1. Read the text aloud several times and in different voices while students listen or follow along silently.
2. Discuss the meaning of the text, as well as your reading of it, with students.
3. Read the text with the class several times, in variations of choral reading. (See Chapter 3 for information on choral reading.)
4. Pair up students and have them take turns reading the text to each other three times each, with the listener offering support and encouragement.
5. Have students reassemble and perform their texts for an audience: their classmates, other classes, school staff, and parents.
6. Ask students to choose two or more words from the text for the classroom word wall and individual word banks. Study the words later through word sorts, games, and practice.
7. Have students put one copy of the text in their poetry folders for later reading at school. Have them take the other copy

> home to read to whoever will listen. The listeners should offer praise and support and sign the back side of the student's text or the Lucky Listeners form on page 154.
>
> 8. Begin the next day with students reading chorally and individually the text from the previous day. Then the routine begins again with a new text.

►Fast Start   *Parents' Role   K–2   adaptable*

Research indicates that parental involvement is key to students' success in learning to read (Henderson, 1988; Padak & Rasinski, 2003). In fact, a recent international study of reading achievement (Postlethwaite & Ross, 1992) found that parental involvement in children's reading was the number-one predictor of reading achievement worldwide. With that in mind, we decided to adapt FDL for parental involvement. The result is a fun instructional program called Fast Start (Padak & Rasinski, 2005, 2008; Rasinski, 1995; Rasinski & Padak, 2004, 2008; Rasinski & Stevenson, 2005).

Fast Start is aimed at students in kindergarten through early second grade, since the parents of those students are more predisposed to be involved in and concerned about reading instruction. We felt that if parents were invited to participate in their children's literacy development early in their school years, they would be more likely to remain involved later on. That said, Fast Start can be easily adapted for children in upper grades.

At the heart of Fast Start is a mantra that has guided much of my work: Good oral reading instruction involves reading to children, reading with children, and listening to children read. That is exactly what we ask parents to do: to devote 15 minutes to doing Fast Start with their children. (See Figure 6.6 on page 155 for guidelines to reproduce for parents.) We provide parents with a text every day—usually a short, lively poem that is printed in a big and bold font, with a large amount of white space for writing on later in the lesson. (See Figure 6.7 on page 156 for a sample.)

Parent and child sit side by side. The parent begins by reading the poem to the child several times, slowly, clearly, and expressively, pointing to the words in the text as he or she reads. After several readings, the child and parent read the poem together aloud, again pointing to the words, as in paired reading. Parent and child should take time throughout the lesson to talk about the poem, its meaning, and their reading of it.

After several paired readings by parent and child, the parent invites the child to read the text to him or her, again pointing to the words as the child reads. The child should read the poem several times. The parent should listen attentively, offer support, and lavish praise on the child for good reading.

The final part of the lesson involves word study because we want children to do more than simply memorize poems. We want them to recognize words from the poems and in other texts they read. Parents can facilitate this in several ways. For example, the child and parent can choose two to four interesting words from the poem and add them to the child's word bank, a collection of words on index cards, or to a home word wall. Those words can be practiced, sorted, and used for a variety of word games such as Bingo, Go Fish, Memory (aka, Concentration), and so forth.

The parent and child can look for rhyming words and key word families (e.g., -at, -ub, -ink) and write them on the photocopy of the poem. Then they can brainstorm and write other words from the same word family. (See Figure 6.8 on page 157 for a sample.) These new words should be read several times and added to the word bank. This is a natural ending point for the lesson—indeed, a lot of reading has occurred! However, since the poem is short, the parent can encourage more repeated reading if the child shows interest.

Informed teachers take advantage of this home reading by putting the poem on the chalkboard or a chart the very next day and engaging students in ten minutes of repeated reading followed by a few minutes of word study. These teachers also periodically send home a Fast Start newsletter with a reading log that reviews the procedures and gives timely tips and encouragement on using the program. (See Figure 6.9 on pages 158–159 for a sample.)

Although it is simple and quick, Fast Start is effective. I found a significant relationship between the use of Fast Start and urban schoolchildren's initial progress in reading over a three-month period (Rasinski, 1995). Parents who used it most often were more likely to see their children make the greatest gains in reading in first grade. Nancy Padak and I found a similar relationship, even when taking into account students' initial differences in reading ability at the beginning of the school year, in a yearlong implementation of Fast Start in another urban school (Rasinski & Padak, 2004). In a study with first-grade students, Bruce Stevenson and I (Rasinski & Stevenson, 2005) found that Fast Start had its greatest impact on children at the most risk for failure to read. These children made two to three times the gains in initial reading compared to students in comparable classrooms who were not receiving Fast Start as an intervention. Fast Start has the potential for closing the gap between the more and less economically advantaged children in beginning reading. It also has the potential to involve parents who might not otherwise be involved in their children's early reading development. The rhymes are so simple that most parents are able to handle them. For those situations where parental literacy is an issue, you can ask a sibling or other family member to help or prerecord the materials for the child to take home.

Frances Imperato, a reading specialist at Martin Luther King Elementary School in Edison, New Jersey, has found similar results with her primary-grade students. She states that Fast Start "is easily administered, shows results, aligns to good teaching, and is enjoyable for both parents and students alike."

➤ Phrased Text Lesson

One of the chief characteristics of the disfluent reader is staccato, word-by-word oral reading. Decoding tends to be so difficult for these readers that they stumble over nearly every word. They do not easily grasp the meaning of phrases because they don't process text in phrasal units. This impacts comprehension greatly because it is the phrase, and not necessarily the word, that carries the weight of the meaning in discourse. To make matters worse, word-by-word reading becomes habitual all too quickly. In my clinical experience, as well as in my observations of many teachers of struggling readers, I have found that once readers get locked into word-by-word reading, it is difficult to move them toward more phrased reading.

In Chapter 4, I discussed the value of having students do repeated reading of high-frequency words in phrases. Another approach for nurturing phrased reading is the phased text lesson (PTL). PTL blends elements of the fluency development lesson, and research evidence shows that we improve students' reading when we provide them with tangible cues to phrase boundaries in text (Rasinski, 1990, 1994). PTL is designed to be taught to individual students or small groups over two consecutive days, 10 to 15 minutes each day. The first day consists of orally reading and rereading phrase-cued texts; the second day is a repeat of the first, but using a conventionally formatted version of the text.

To prepare, select short reading passages and mark or "cue" phrase boundaries for the reader. (See Figure 6.10 on page 160 for an example of phrase-cued text.) I generally choose 100-word segments from texts students have recently read or will read in the near future. With a pencil, I mark phrase boundaries with slash marks—single slashes for within-sentence boundaries (indicating a short pause) and double slashes for sentence boundaries (indicating a longer pause). There are no hard-and-fast rules for cueing texts; you just need to trust your judgment. I've found that, although teachers' marks may not correlate perfectly on a particular text, the level of agreement among them is highly consistent.

On the first day of using PTL, make a copy of the phrase-cued text for each student. Begin the lesson by passing out the text to students, discussing the importance of reading in phrasal units and explaining the purpose of the marks on the text. From there, read the text to the students a few times, emphasizing and slightly exaggerating the phrases. Then read the text chorally with students (oral support) a few times, in meaningful phrases. Finally, ask students to pair up for two to three rounds of repeated reading. End day one of PTL by having students perform their text for the group. Students are often amazed at how fluent and meaningful their reading has become.

On the next day, repeat everything you did the day before but use the original text without phrase boundaries. This helps students transfer the knowledge they gained using phrase-cued text to conventionally formatted text. Over time, students develop their understanding of how texts are phrased and apply that understanding to new, never-before-seen passages. (See page 153 for step-by-step guidelines on teaching the PTL lesson.)

For students locked into word-by-word reading, PTL offers hope. Sally Herman, a Title I teacher, claims that the PTL works where other approaches have not: "I have found it very difficult to get students away from the word-bound reading once they get into it. The PTL is a great way to help kids read faster and, more important, in meaningful phrases and word groups. In as little as two or three weeks of instruction, many students are experiencing success."

PTL is designed to be taught to individual students or small groups, over two consecutive days, 10 to 15 minutes each day.

Day 1
1. Give each student a copy of a phrased-cued text, similar to the one in Figure 6.10.
2. Remind students of the importance of reading in phrases, not word by word.
3. Explain the purpose of the phrase markings on the text.
4. Read the text to students several times, emphasizing and slightly exaggerating the phrases.
5. Read the text with students two or three times in a choral fashion, emphasizing good phrasing and expression.
6. Have students read the text orally with a partner, two or three readings per student.
7. Have students perform the text orally for the group.

Day 2
Repeat the procedure from the first day, using the same text *but without the phrase boundaries marked* to help students transfer their understanding of phrased reading to conventional text.

➤Concluding Thoughts

Try out these synergistic lessons and see how they work for you. If they are effective, continue to use them and modify them to meet your needs, the needs of your students, and the teaching and learning style that characterizes your classroom. If, on the other hand, the lessons don't work for you, create your own based on your informed knowledge of these strategies and how to apply and combine them. Remember, in instruction, the whole, when created from a logical combination of good practices, is greater than the sum of the parts.

Figure 6.5

Name: _____

LUCKY LISTENERS

Directions: Read your poem to someone at school or at home. Then ask that person to add his or her name to this form and the date and time of the reading. Your listener should write what they liked about the poem and how you read it. If your lucky listener listens more than once, he or she can sign the form for each time. Even your pets can listen to you read (think of ways that they can sign their names to the form). Try to get at least five signatures.

Title of Poem: _____

Lucky Listener's Name	Date and Time of Reading	Comments on the Poem and Your Reading

Scholastic Teaching Resources   *The Fluent Reader*

Figure 6.6

Dear Parents:

Fast Start is a fun program designed to build your child's reading skills. You spend no more than 15 minutes reading, rereading, and teaching a different poem to your child each day. The poem is printed on a sheet of paper with plenty of white space for you to write on later. Here's all you have to do:

1. Sit side by side with your child and read the poem to him or her several times through, with good expression. Be sure to point to the words as you read so that your child connects the spoken words to the printed words.

2. Read aloud the poem together and point to the words, as in step one. Talk about the poem and how well you read it.

3. After reading the poem several times together, invite your child to read the poem several times to you. Listen attentively, offer support, and lavish praise on your child for good reading.

4. Engage in word study:

   a. With your child, choose two to four interesting words from the poem and add them to your child's word bank (e.g., a collection of words on index cards) and/or to a home word wall. Practice and sort the words in various categories. Use them for word games such as Bingo, Go Fish, Memory (aka, Concentration), and so forth.

   b. Look for rhyming words and key word families (e.g., *-at, -ub, -ink*) and write them on the photocopy of the poem. Then brainstorm and write down other rhyming words or words from the same family. Read these words several times and add them to the word bank.

5. In school the following day, I will put the poem on the chalkboard or a chart and read it with students several times. I will also talk to students about what they learned at home from the reading and engage them in more word study, focusing on word families and sight words—words that should be recognized instantly, on sight, with no analysis or decoding.

Thanks for your participation!

Scholastic Teaching Resources *The Fluent Reader*

Fast Start Rhyme

JACK AND JILL

Jack and Jill went up the hill

To fetch a pail of water.

Jack fell down and broke his crown,

And Jill came tumbling after.

Up Jack got and home did trot

As fast as he could caper;

And went to bed to mend his head

With vinegar and brown paper.

Scholastic Teaching Resources   *The Fluent Reader*

Figure 6.8

LIST WORD FAMILIES AND WORDS FROM "JACK AND JILL"

-ill	-own	-ot	-er	-ed/-ead
Jill	crown	got	caper	bed
hill	down	trot	paper	head
mill	brown	hot	her	bread
spill	frown	spot	gerbil	shed
skill	town	dot	jumper	sled

JACK AND JILL

Jack and (Jill) went up the (hill)

To fetch a pail of water.

Jack fell <u>down</u> and broke his <u>crown</u>,

And (Jill) came tumbling after.

Up Jack |got| and home did |trot|

As fast as he could caper;

And went to bed to mend his head

With vinegar and <u>brown</u> paper.

Figure 6.9

September Fast Start Reading Newsletter

"Read to Your Child, Read With Your Child, Listen to Your Child Read"
Abraham Lincoln Elementary School

Dear Parents:

We are beginning another year of Fast Start Reading at Lincoln Elementary School in kindergarten through grade 2 and invite you to participate in your son's or daughter's reading development.

Fast Start is a simple, 10-to-15 minute per day, read-at-home program that research has shown helps children develop reading skills. Every Monday, your child will bring home a packet of Fast Start poems or other short passages. Simply pick a convenient and quiet time for Fast Start Reading. Sit next to your child at the kitchen table, couch, or other comfortable spot and read the assigned passage several times this way:

- Read the passage to your child several times. Point to the words as they are read.
- Read the passage aloud with your child several times. This time, have your child point to the words as they are read by the two of you.
- Invite your child to read the passage to you, once, twice, or three times. Ask your child to point to words as they are read. Provide whatever help your child may need and praise your son or daughter for their good work in reading the passage.
- Do some word activities with your child for a few minutes, such as finding and underlining particular words in the passage, finding and writing other words that rhyme with some of the words in the passage, adding two or three words from each passage to a deck of flashcards that you and your child develop, or playing word games with your child using the words from the flashcards. In next month's newsletter we will share with you ideas for doing word study activities with your child.

Fast Start Reading should take no more than 15 minutes per day. Your child will love spending the time with you and learning how to read the passages. And your child's teacher will begin each morning by reading that same passage from the night before with the children to give them extra practice. Please complete the attached Fast Start Reading Log for each reading.

Research has shown that, when done on a regular basis, Fast Start Reading helps children develop as readers faster than if they receive reading instruction only at school.

Please be sure to attend one of the upcoming Fast Start Reading training sessions at Lincoln School with your child. Here are the times we are offering a brief, one-hour training that will show you how best to do Fast Start Reading with your child.

Monday, September 9: (3 sessions) 8:00 a.m., 3:00 p.m., 6:00 p.m. Room 101.
Tuesday, September 10: (3 sessions) 8:00 a.m., 3:00 p.m., 7:00 p.m. Room 101.
Thursday, September 12: (3 sessions) 8:00 a.m., 3:00 p.m., 7:00 p.m. Room 101.

Refreshments will be served. Remember, you only need to attend one of the above training sessions.

Scholastic Teaching Resources   *The Fluent Reader*

Fast Start Reading Log

(Figure 6.9, continued)

Student's Name: _____ **Week of:** _____

Please return this log to your teacher every Monday morning.

Day	Passage/ Poem to Read	Minutes Spent in Fast Start Reading	Parent's Comments	Child's Comments
Monday				
Tuesday				
Wednesday				
Thursday				
Friday				
Saturday				
Sunday				

Remember to read to your child, read with your child, and listen to your child read. Then study and play with the words in the passage or poem. Good luck—and have fun!

Scholastic Teaching Resources   *The Fluent Reader*

Figure 6.10

Examples of Phrase-Cued Texts

Four score and seven years ago / our fathers brought forth / on this continent, / a new nation, / conceived in Liberty, / and dedicated to the proposition / that all men are created equal. //

Now we are engaged / in a great civil war, / testing whether that nation, / or any nation so conceived / and so dedicated, / can long endure. // We are met on a great battlefield of that war. // We have come to dedicate a portion of that field, / as a final resting place / for those who here / gave their lives / that that nation might live. // It is altogether fitting and proper / that we should do this. //

Excerpt from the *Gettysburg Address*

Today, / there is a park / in Hiroshima / where the bomb dropped. // Near the park / is a museum. // It opened in 1955 / and houses / some 6000 items / left after the explosion. //

Each year / 1,200,000 people / visit the museum. // They look / at the photos and exhibits. // And / they examine / the twisted roof tiles / and melted bottles. // They are / strange disturbing relics / of that terrible moment. //

Japan has built / a new wing / to the museum. // The new exhibit / includes Japan's role in World War II / and shows / how the city of Hiroshima / participated in the military effort. // For the first time, / the bombing is placed / in a historical context. //

From *Hiroshima* by Laurence Yep. Copyright © 1995 by Laurence Yep. Reprinted by permission of Scholastic Inc.

Chapter 7

Oral Reading Within and Across the School Curriculum

Making Reading Fluency an Everyday Classroom Experience

"I surrendered to a world of my imagination, reenacting all those wonderful tales my father would read aloud to me. I became a very active reader, especially history and Shakespeare."

——Andrew Wyeth, American artist

To this point, I've presented many ideas, activities, and lessons for oral reading, but without much consideration for how to fit them into day-to-day classroom teaching. You may be asking yourself, "How do I weave oral reading into my curriculum in ways that don't take time away from other activities, but rather complement and help me to extend those activities?" Only you, the teacher, knows the answer to that question. This is another instance of the science of teaching reading coming face to face with the art of teaching reading. Only you know your goals for instruction. Only you know your style of teaching. Only you know the strengths and weaknesses of your students. And only you can make the final decision on how oral reading should play out in your classroom.

That said, this chapter presents examples of ways to assist you in making oral reading a regular part of your daily routine. A lot of the strategies will seem familiar because I presented them in detail in previous chapters. However, I organize them differently here to give you a better sense of how they might play out in the classroom on a regular basis. Specifically, I discuss oral reading activities and routines that can be:

- **done daily for their own sake**, independent of any curriculum area.
- **integrated into the general reading curriculum** to coexist nicely with your basal or literature-based guided reading program.
- **integrated into the content areas** to not only build literacy skills, but also knowledge in math, science, social studies, art, music, and physical education.
- **done at home with parents and other family members** to promote healthy home-school partnerships and aid parents in helping their children become better readers.

A couple of caveats are in order. First, it would be physically impossible to implement all the activities and routines covered in this chapter. I present ideas and suggestions I have garnered from a variety of teachers; they are not the work of any one teacher. Second, these activities and routines are only models of ways you can implement oral reading on your own. Whether you use any of the ideas here or develop your own routines, remember that oral reading can and should play an important part in students' reading development. It should be an integral part of your reading curriculum.

▶Implementing Daily Oral Reading Routines

Classroom routines are so important because they provide structure for students. Some routines are best done on a monthly basis, some on a weekly basis, and others on a daily basis. Following are oral reading routines that, in my opinion, should be carried out every day.

Teacher-Led Read Aloud

It probably comes as no surprise to you that I include read aloud as an essential, everyday oral reading activity. It is an activity that has too many benefits to attribute to any one area of the curriculum. By reading to students, we share our own enthusiasm for reading. We model good, meaningful, and fluent reading (especially when we talk with students about how our own oral reading was fluent and what made it fluent); we build students' vocabulary and, if we show students the text as we read, we're likely to build their word recognition skills, too. We strengthen comprehension by reading sophisticated texts—texts that students couldn't handle on their own. We teach students the structures of well-formed stories; we expose them to genres that they may not read on their own; and we share information about their cultures, as well as the cultures of other people around the world. Clearly, there is much to be gained from read aloud. It deserves to stand on its own.

Find a special time of day to devote to read aloud, a time when the class is in a reflective mood—before or after lunch, after a recess, or near the end of the day are all good times. Make the time inviolate; whether you read aloud for 10 minutes or 30 minutes per day, do not let other activities encroach. Begin and end with a ritual, such as reciting a favorite poem. Use read aloud to develop knowledge and skills: Discuss and collect interesting words from the text. Have students write about the read aloud in their journals. Use the books you read as stepping-stones to other books by the same author or on similar topics. Make those books available to your students. (For more information on read aloud, see Chapter 2.)

Poetry Reading

Poetry touches the heart as well as the mind. Reading it is a wonderful way to develop students' literacy skills, as well as their love of literature. Students delight in the words, phrases, and various literary devices of poems. Because it is meant to be read aloud, with all its rhyme, rhythm, and repetition fully articulated, poetry is a natural for building reading fluency. Just as teacher-led read aloud should be a regular part of all elementary and middle school curricula, so should poetry reading. However, it is a genre that is all too often neglected.

If you believe poetry is worth teaching, then a poetry coffeehouse is worth trying in your classroom. Not only does it develop a love of poetry in students, but it also provides an authentic context for repeated reading that will no doubt have a positive effect on students' literacy learning. Moreover, a poetry coffeehouse takes a minimal amount of time and effort to implement. For a small investment, the poetry coffeehouse is an effective way to make oral reading instruction and poetry appreciation work in your classroom. (For more information on reading and performing poetry, see Chapter 5.)

Fluency Development Lesson

Are you a first-, second- or third-grade teacher with a class largely composed of students who have difficulty in fluency? Or perhaps a Title I reading teacher who works with small groups of struggling readers? Or maybe a sixth-grade teacher with a handful of students who read in a slow, word-by-word manner? If so, then the fluency development lesson (FDL) may make a wonderful stand-alone component of your reading curriculum. FDL is an intense daily instructional routine that can have a powerful, dramatic effect on students' growth in fluency and overall reading achievement.

In some primary-grade classrooms, FDL is often used as a daily warm-up activity. Other teachers employ it regularly before or after lunch. One teacher I know uses it as the start of guided reading with her struggling readers. At my university's reading clinic, we use an adapted version of FDL as one of our core lessons for students who are diagnosed with problems in word decoding and fluency. The phrased text lesson (PTL), another good activity for building fluency, can be implemented under similar circumstances. (For more information on FDL and PTL, see Chapter 6.)

►Integrating Oral Reading Into the General Reading Curriculum

A balanced reading program should feature both oral and silent reading, with a strong emphasis on oral reading in the early grades. As students mature, it usually makes sense to reduce the amount of oral reading they do. However, some form of it should remain a regular feature, even in the middle grades. There are many ways to make oral reading an integral part of your existing reading curriculum, beyond round robin reading. Below are a few suggestions.

Radio Reading

Radio reading is a good antidote to round robin reading. It can be integrated easily into regular classroom instruction; for example, as an extension of guided reading. In most classrooms, guided reading is structured around a common text that is read and discussed in small groups. Typically, radio reading kicks in after the initial silent reading and discussion of the text. The teacher assigns segments of the text to individual group members. Students practice the text on their own and develop comprehension questions based on it. The next time the group meets, students perform their reading as clearly and expressively as possible, as if they were professional actors or announcers. The reading is followed by a discussion based on the questions students developed. After the performance and discussion, students move on to the next story or the next section of the story they had been reading. (For more information on radio reading, see Chapter 4.)

Oral Recitation Lesson and Fluency Oriented Reading Instruction

Unlike radio reading, which is typically used as a component of guided reading, the oral recitation lesson (ORL) (Hoffman, 1987) and fluency oriented reading instruction (FORI) (Stahl & Heubach, 2005; Kuhn et al., 2006) are complete guided reading lessons in and of themselves that can easily be integrated into an existing reading program. Students work their way through a series of texts, focusing on comprehension and summarization, as well as oral reading fluency.

For individual students or small groups of students struggling in fluency and comprehension, ORL and FORI are proven interventions that can be used daily over an extended period of time. Or they can be implemented occasionally, as an alternative to other forms of guided reading instruction. (For more information on ORL and FORI, see Chapter 6.)

Paired Reading

Paired reading is another approach to oral reading that may complement your guided reading program well. After introducing a story to be read, pair students up and ask them to read the text aloud simultaneously or use some other supported form of reading, such as echo reading or shared reading. You can also ask pairs of students to read the text aloud together after they read it on their own, silently. Assigning reading this way makes students responsible not only for their own reading and comprehension, but also for that of their partner. (For more information on paired reading, see Chapter 3.)

Choral Reading

Like paired reading, choral reading adds variety to guided reading and provides oral reading support, but it also builds classroom community because of its very nature. Groups of students read the same text aloud in various ways, expressively and cooperatively. As a matter of procedure, some teachers begin the reading of an assigned text in a choral fashion, discuss the passage with the group, and then ask students to read the remainder of the text silently. (For more information on choral reading, see Chapter 3.)

Reading While Listening

With so many great books and instructional materials for children out there, it would take a miracle worker to make it through all of them. But does every text have to be read in the same way and with the same intensity? Of course not. You may wish to explore some texts in great depth. You may cover others in a faster, more efficient manner. Reading while listening is one way to move quickly through a text and still help students make major gains in their reading fluency and their overall reading development.

One way to do the activity is by reading aloud the text to students as they follow along in individual copies of the text, pointing to lines as you read them and stopping from time to time to ask questions or make comments. Once this form of assisted reading is complete, engage students in a follow-up discussion and extension activities that you normally assign after reading a story.

Reading while listening has positive consequences. Your read aloud provides a meaningful model of expressive, fluent reading and shows variety in the way the reading is done. Sixth-grade teacher Kathy Kalkbrenner notes that her students love to read passages silently as she reads them orally. "I know they're reading because they follow along in their books. I think their comprehension improves since they don't have to worry about sounding out unknown words. Best of all, I think this helps them discover just how a good reader reads. I've been told on more than one occasion, by more than one student, 'Gee, Mrs. K., I wish I could read like you.'" (For more information on assisted reading and reading while listening, see Chapter 3.)

Reading-Listening Centers

Another way to integrate assisted reading into the regular curriculum is to develop a reading-listening center. On their daily visits to the center, students are expected to spend 15–20 minutes reading a selected book, poem, or passage while listening to a prerecorded version of it. Students practice the reading and listening until they are able to read the passage independently to the teacher (or other adult checker) without assistance. The assisted and repeated reading involved in this practice will go a long way to develop general reading fluency and a sense of reading mastery in students.

As I mentioned in Chapter 3, a reading-listening center can be stocked with printed and recorded materials that are purchased commercially. The recordings, however, can also be made by the teacher, adult volunteers, or other students in or out of your own classroom. The use of technology and podcasting has made the classroom development of a reading-listening center even more feasible. Once students become familiar with your expectations for them and the routine for using the center daily, the reading-listening center can largely run independently with minimal intervention from you, the teacher.

Readers' Theater in the Literacy Program

Most reading scholars agree that reading response, the activity one does after reading a text to consolidate his or her understanding of it, is essential to comprehension. Reading response can take a variety of forms, from writing in a response journal to engaging in a group discussion to creating an artistic representation of the text's major themes.

Another form of response is recasting a guided reading text as a script, practicing the script, and performing it as readers' theater. Writing the script is a strong scaffolded experience because it requires students to delve deeply into the original text. Practicing and performing the script are also strong scaffolded experiences because they lead students to serious consideration of the text while developing their fluency and word recognition skills—and most students love to perform. Readers' theater is a simple yet powerful way to make performance reading an integral part of your reading curriculum.

For one week, Sandy Thomas devoted her read-aloud time to the funny, ironic stories of Robert Munsch. At the end of the week, she asked students to get into groups, choose a Munsch story, and respond to it in a creative, meaningful way. Two groups created artistic representations of the text. Another group turned their story into a game. However, the group that received the most accolades transformed their story, *The Paper Bag Princess* (Munsch, 1980), into a short script, practiced it over several days, and then performed it for their classmates. The students received such a warm response that they took the script "on the road" and performed it in other classrooms, as well as at the retirement village down the road, at a PTA meeting, and, finally, at a local school board meeting. Interestingly, the group was made up mostly of poor readers. However, because they had been performing readers' theater scripts often in class, they were eager to create a script themselves and read it for others. (For more information on readers' theater, see Chapter 5.)

➤ Integrating Oral Reading Into the Content Areas

Is oral reading applicable and useful in science, social studies, art, and other areas of the elementary and middle school curriculum? The answer, of course, is a resounding yes. Here are a few suggestions for integrating it across the curriculum.

Readers' Theater Beyond the Literacy Program

Creative teachers make essential information and ideas tangible to students. Turning content area texts and concepts into readers' theater scripts is one way to do that.

In Chapter 5, I shared the stories of two science teachers whose students became cells and planets in readers' theater performances. The same creativity can be applied in other areas. Imagine a math class, for example, where students create and perform a script featuring prime numbers or geometric shapes as characters. Consider other areas of the curriculum in which students can use readers' theater to reenact famous events from art, music, sports, or history. Think about a social studies curriculum in which famous scenes from history are revisited through readers' theater. Or picture performances in which difficult social interactions, such as racism or bullying, are portrayed and later discussed in class. Activities such as these do happen in classrooms across the country, just not frequently enough.

Mary Smith, a fifth/sixth-grade teacher, finds readers' theater a superb vehicle for student research in social studies.

> *"After reading about a historical event, I have students work in groups of four to six to develop a short script on some aspect of the event. They have to learn more about the characters and facts in order to create a believable script—and that's research. They dig into books, encyclopedias, the Internet. They talk with their parents and people who might know something about their topic. Then, they have to integrate their collective knowledge into a script—that's writing and communication. Finally, they have to practice and perform their scripts—that's reading."*

In Mary's class, students recreated the discussion that may have taken place in the Virginia state assembly in 1861 as legislators debated whether to secede from the Union. They explored the thoughts of South Carolina slaves considering running away and finding their way to freedom on the Underground Railroad. They investigated the modern-day topic of how citizens get laws passed at local, state, and national levels. And they did all of this by creating, practicing, and performing readers' theater scripts. According to Mary:

"When students can create scripts on topics like these, they demonstrate a deep level of understanding, they make history and social studies interesting, and they teach classmates who make up their audience. I used to think activities like readers' theater were just for fun. Activities we could do when all the real work was done. I know now that I was wrong—at least partially wrong. Readers' theater is fun, a lot of fun, but it also makes for good teaching and good learning."

Developing scripts this way takes work, but it's productive work. It takes time to practice the script before performing it, but it's productive time. Moreover, once the script is created, you can use it in future classes. (For more information on readers' theater, see Chapter 5.)

Middle school teacher Kim Hurst writes parodies to songs, raps, and poems to help her students learn earth science content. However, when her students orally practice and perform the parodies, they are also working on their reading fluency in a most engaging way. Below is a parody that Kim wrote for learning about rocks!

Geology will ROCK YOU!!!!!

2X = Geology will ROCK YOU!

(Verse 1: Igneous)
The first group of rocks we cover is a must . . .
Made from lava & magma it is ig-ne-ous.
Intrusive or ex—it depends on where it cooled
There's obsidian and granite—just to name a few . . .

2X = Geology will ROCK YOU!

(Verse 2: Sedimentary)
The second group of rocks is sediment-tar-y
Formed from tiny sediments that were carried.
They were compacted & cemented over time
Conglomerate & sandstone are ones you can find.

2X = Geology will ROCK YOU!

(Verse 3: Metamorphic)
The last group of rocks are meta-mor-phic
That heat & pressure always does the trick.
It's when one type of rock turns into another
Foliated or non—gneiss and marble are others.

2X = Geology will ROCK YOU!

(Verse 4: Rock Cycle)
Now you may be thinkin' that they stay the same,
But they change composition & they change their name.
Earth's processes are so incred-i-ble . . .
We call these changes "the rock cycle."

2X = Geology will ROCK YOU!

Performance Reading of Speeches and Poems

History is marked by speeches and poems that commemorate famous events. Reading these speeches and poems helps students master essential content. These pieces of literature add depth, texture, and variety to any history curriculum.

While celebrating the accomplishments of women during Women's History Month, one seventh-grade teacher, Julie Dixon, had her students practice and perform Sojourner Truth's speech "Ain't I a Woman?"

> *"I gave the students a week to prepare. Some practiced and performed the speech individually; others planned out their performance in duets and trios, doing choral and solo reading. On Monday afternoon, they read their speeches. It was amazing. Even though the same speech was read again and again, each performance was slightly different. The students were captivated by the powerful words of Sojourner Truth. Afterwards, we talked about the performances. The students agreed that if we had just read the speech silently, it would not have had the same impact. Some things are meant to be read orally. The speech had such an impact on my students that, even months later, they were asking rhetorically, 'Ain't I a kid?' 'Ain't I a reader?' 'Ain't I a student?'"*

I don't suggest asking students to memorize speeches and poems. People who give speeches and recite poetry often have their text in front of them when they perform for an audience. Students should be given permission to do the same. Remember, speeches and poems are meant to be read orally. Their meaning is not just in the words, but also in the oral interpretation of those words. So students' time would be better spent practicing speeches and poems, rather than memorizing them, to make them come alive for the audience. (For more information on performance reading of speeches and poems, see Chapter 5.)

Recorded Reading Material

Content area reading material is often too difficult for students who struggle, and many students benefit from oral reading support. One of the easiest ways to deliver such support is through prerecorded texts. Record the reading assignment on tape and have the student listen to it while reading a print version of the text at the same time. By doing this, struggling students benefit in two ways: They improve their reading skills, and they learn the assigned content.

Sixth-grade teacher Kathy Kalkbrenner says that many of her students have difficulty with their textbooks. Yet she must cover the content.

> *"We have specific content that needs to be covered. And I can't go out and get new, easier books for them to read that cover the same content. So I will read one chapter at a time and record it on a cassette tape. I will also embed some of my own thoughts and questions into the tape as I read. Then, I place the tape in the listening area. Groups of students go to the area and read the book as they listen to the text. I usually have to remind them to follow along in the book as they listen. Most do. Even some of my better students like to listen to the chapter tapes, sometimes before and sometimes after they read the chapter on their own. They say it helps their learning. It's a great example for students who are somewhat behind."*

Developing the recordings may take a bit of time and effort. However, once they're made, your work is pretty much done. If you create podcasts of the recordings, you can duplicate them, e-mail them home, post them on your classroom Web site, place them in a reading-listening center (see page 167), and use them as much as you like, for as long as you like. You can also enlist the help of better readers in the class to make the recordings for you. (For more information on prerecorded reading material, see Chapter 3.)

➤ Bringing Oral Reading Into the Home

Oral reading often comes naturally to parents. In many homes, it is already an everyday event. When bedtime stories are shared, scout mottos are practiced, or interesting passages from the newspaper are passed across the breakfast table, families are engaging in oral reading. As educators, we have powerful, easy-to-implement oral reading activities that can assist parents in helping their children learn to read. We need to make ongoing, concerted efforts to educate parents about the critical role they can play and give them the tools to carry out that role effectively and enjoyably. Here are some ways to make oral reading work even more effectively at home.

Parent Read Aloud

In her seminal study, Dolores Durkin (1966) found that the children who learned to read earliest came from homes in which parents read to them daily and in such a way that the children could see the text. Parent read aloud—or sharing a book for the sheer pleasure of it—is not only a natural parent-child activity but also a great way to develop readers.

In many families, though, reading aloud ends once formal schooling begins. This is unfortunate, because children receive the same benefits when their parents read to them as they receive when their teacher reads to them—improved vocabulary, comprehension, motivation to read, and so forth. (For more information on teacher-led read aloud, see Chapter 2.) Regardless of the grade we teach, we need to make reading to children a priority for parents. In addition to reading in a fluid, expressive, and engaging manner, parents need to be reminded to make sure that their children track the text visually while they listen to their parents read.

Paired Reading

Paired reading, which involves two readers reading one text orally together, was originally developed by Keith Topping as a way for parents to tutor their children. Research by Topping and others found that as little as 10 or 15 minutes per day of paired reading between a parent and child resulted in significant improvement in the child's reading.

Paired reading is a natural activity to encourage parents to do. At two Akron, Ohio, city schools, Barrett and Robinson, paired reading is central to parent involvement. It's easy, quick, and effective. In an hour-long workshop, teachers train parents how to do paired reading with their children, as follows.

- Find a daily 10- to15-minute period to do paired reading with your child.
- Sit comfortably next to your child. Allow your child to choose a text to read (assigned reading, pleasure reading, etc.).
- You and your child read the text aloud together; have your child point to the text as it is read. Adjust your reading speed so that it is a comfortable fit with your child.
- If your child wishes to try reading alone, have him or her give you a signal (e.g., soft tap on the hand) to stop reading. Continue to follow along silently as your child reads.
- If your child has difficulty with a particular word, simply state the word, have your child say it aloud, and then continue reading aloud together.
- After 10 to 15 minutes, stop reading and talk about what you read and how it was read (e.g., any difficult areas, any words that the child had difficulty with).

Imagine what might happen if every parent of a primary-grade child read to his or her child for ten minutes every day and then they read together (paired reading) for another ten minutes. I suspect literacy levels in this country would be much higher. (For more information on paired reading, see Chapter 3.)

Fast Start

A synergistic activity that incorporates elements of read aloud, paired reading, and repeated reading, Fast Start (Padak & Rasinski, 2005, 2008) is intended for use by parents with children in the primary grades. It is a simple way to move students from read aloud to independent reading. Several studies have demonstrated its ease and effectiveness, as well as the fact that parents and children enjoy and appreciate the opportunity to read together at home.

Although Fast Start was developed for use with primary-grade students, it can easily be adapted for older students who struggle in reading by choosing texts at their instructional level. (For more information on Fast Start, see Chapter 6.)

The Case for Silent Reading Fluency

The ultimate goal of this book is to help teachers improve students' reading comprehension and overall reading proficiency through fluency instruction. Fluency in reading is normally associated with oral reading. Fluent reading is normally heard. Thus, most of this book has been aimed at teaching fluency through oral reading methods. However, because silent reading is such a ubiquitous form of reading beyond the elementary grades, instruction in oral reading is worthwhile largely to the extent that it can positively impact readers' silent reading comprehension.

Implied throughout this book is the assumption that improvements in oral reading fluency will also yield improvements in silent reading proficiency (Rasinski, 2006). Oral reading and silent reading are closely related. Improvements in one should result in gains in the other. Indeed, much of the research on fluency instruction that I have shared in this book has also demonstrated improvements in silent reading.

However, two obvious questions must be raised at this point:

1. Is there such a thing as silent reading fluency?
2. If so, can silent reading fluency be taught directly through silent reading practice?

I think that both questions can be answered in the affirmative. The same processes that are the basis for oral reading fluency—accuracy and automaticity in word recognition and the ability to phrase text into meaningful units—are essential elements in silent reading. Surely, silent reading requires readers to accurately and effortlessly identify the words in the text. Moreover, in silent reading, readers need to group words into meaningful phrasal units. Even while reading silently, most readers report hearing their voice, and this voice helps them in phrasing the text and in making meaning. In oral reading, these processes are clearly obvious through the oral rendering of a passage. In silent reading, they lie beneath the surface, as they cannot be directly observed or heard by an outside observer. Still, these processes are present in silent reading: Fluency is required for proficient silent reading.

Earlier in this book, I stated that oral reading fluency is achieved through practice. Through wide, repeated, and assisted oral reading, students develop fluency in their reading. Again, it seems logical that fluency in silent reading can (and should) also be nurtured through plenty of practice in silent reading (Worthy & Broaddus, 2001/2002).

Silent reading is particularly important for the reading curriculum (as well as reading done in the content areas) because oral reading instruction does pose some serious practical limitations in the classroom. Since oral reading is not as common a form of reading as silent reading is beyond the primary grades, oral reading may not have the same degree of authenticity as silent reading. In group instructional settings, oral reading is most often done one student at a time; other students in the group usually do not read while another student is reading. Efficiency in the use of time for reading is thus diminished. In addition, oral reading by one student may cause disruptions for other students. Listening to classmates reading orally may cause students to become distracted and make them devote less attention to their own reading or learning task. Finally, by the upper elementary and middle grades, fear and embarrassment as a result of miscues made while reading orally can further diminish the effectiveness of oral reading activities and students' confidence in their own reading. These limitations beg the question then: Is it possible to promote fluency in reading, and thereby improve comprehension through silent reading instruction?

Although it would seem to be reasonable to infer that silent reading practice would improve reading fluency and overall reading achievement—and correlational studies have shown that students who read more (silently or orally) tend to be better readers, while students who read less tend to rank lower in reading achievement and reading progress—this inference is not supported by existing research. The National Reading Panel's (2000) review of the research indicated that there was not clear and convincing evidence through empirical research that having students read silently actually leads to improved reading performance. Thus, in many schools, the NRP's finding has been interpreted as a mandate that silent reading activities in schools should be abandoned, and activities such as sustained silent reading have been eliminated from many school programs.

Teaching Silent Reading Fluency

Rather than abandoning silent reading, we really need to step back and ask ourselves why the experimental evidence to support silent reading is so lean. Surely, it makes sense that reading, whether orally or silently, should make one a better reader. I am convinced that practice does make one a better reader. In many cases where students were given the opportunity to practice silent reading, there was actually little reading going on. My colleague and fourth-grade teacher Lorraine Griffith calls it "fake reading." Any close observer of sustained silent reading (SSR), during which the teacher is either reading on his or her own or engaged in some other activity, will find that many students are not really reading. You will find students looking at a book without really reading it, choosing books that are much too difficult or too easy, frequently changing books during the SSR period, chatting with a friend or two, walking aimlessly around the room, or doing something other than reading during this period. If students are not really reading during SSR, there is no reason to expect them to improve.

The lack of structure and accountability is one problem. The lack of support for students is another. My friend and colleague Ray Reutzel uses the analogy of learning to drive a car. Few drivers would be successful in learning to drive a car if, during drivers' education, the teacher did the following:

- Modeled driving an automobile while students watched from a distance
- Allowed students to drive without any instruction prior to driving
- Allowed students to choose their own vehicles in which to learn to drive
- Allowed students to drive independently while the teacher remained in his or her office working on other tasks
- Did not hold students accountable for their actions while driving

Ray notes that similar conditions exist in many SSR periods, during which the teacher gives little guidance or support to students in the following areas: selecting appropriate materials, providing instruction on how to read independently, holding students accountable for the time spent reading, and doing little more than modeling the act of reading during SSR. He argues compellingly that we should not expect students to gain much from that form of silent reading—there is little direct instruction provided by teachers and little accountability for students for the precious instructional time that is given over for SSR.

Reutzel and his colleagues (Reutzel, Jones, Fawson, & Smith, 2008) propose an alternative to SSR that they call scaffolded silent reading (ScSR). In ScSR, students are given the opportunity to read independently but under more controlled conditions than those found in SSR: The teacher plays a more active instructional role, and students are held more accountable for their time. Specific features of ScSR that are not found in SSR include the following:

- The teacher instructs and models appropriate book selection strategies for students.
- Books and reading materials for ScSR are stored and organized around genres and clearly identified by difficulty level.
- Although students have choices in what they may select for ScSR, it is limited by the teacher as to text difficulty (at their independent reading level) and genre. (We want to insure that students read a wide range of genres and don't limit themselves to one type of reading).
- Students are held accountable for reading during ScSR by the teacher visually monitoring them and engaging in five-minute conferences with them. Students are also asked to set personal goals for their reading, periodically read to the teacher and answer questions about their reading, and complete one or more book response activity after completing a book.

In a yearlong study of ScSR in four third-grade classrooms, Reutzel and his colleagues found that students using ScSR made substantial gains in various aspects of their reading (word recognition, fluency, and comprehension). Moreover, these gains were statistically similar to the gains found in students who engaged in oral and guided repeated readings of passages. Thus, this approach to silent reading fluency, in which students are given support and assistance in their silent reading and held accountable for their time, seems to foster similar positive results as oral reading fluency instruction.

My colleagues and I (Rasinski, Samuels, Hiebert, Petscher, & Feller, in press) also examined the impact of a silent reading instructional protocol called reading plus (RP), designed to improve reading proficiency through silent reading fluency practice in students in grades 4 through 10. The RP intervention involves students in a series of online lessons, each approximately 30 minutes in length. The heart of each lesson is a structured sustained silent reading activity for which students read texts chosen from a range of engaging selections at their instructional reading level. Lesson text is presented in either a guided or an independent manner, each within controlled presentation formats and rate parameters. A set of comprehension questions follows each reading selection. The texts become progressively more challenging, and the speed at which the text is presented is incrementally increased as students move through the program. Each lesson also contains a visual perceptual activity, a cloze reading task, and a vocabulary activity. Essentially, the technology in the program is designed to provide sufficient structure and assistance for students to be successful on appropriately challenging reading materials and, by constantly monitoring students' performance, it holds them accountable for their time spent reading. In a large urban district where reading achievement has been substantially below the state norm and standards, a yearlong intervention study using RP found positive, substantial, and significant improvements in students' reading comprehension and overall reading achievement. These improvements were reported on both criteria-referenced and norm-referenced tests of reading comprehension and achievement for students in grades 4 through 10. Students in the RP silent reading fluency intervention made gains in reading that were significantly greater than students enrolled in alternative intervention programs. Moreover, the average gains made by students in the RP intervention were greater than the average gains for all students at the state and district levels.

This study, as well as the study by Reutzel and his colleagues (Reutzel et al., 2008), suggests that reading achievement can be improved through silent reading fluency methods. As with oral reading fluency, the keys to success in silent reading appear to be: providing students with appropriately challenging and interesting materials; offering sufficient structure, support, and assistance for students to be successful; giving students opportunities to engage in actual context reading (wide reading as well as repeated reading); and ensuring that students are actually engaged in reading during the allotted time by monitoring their performance and holding them accountable for their reading.

➤Concluding Thoughts

In this chapter, I provided a sampling of the many ways in which you, the informed teacher, can incorporate oral (and silent) reading fluency instruction into all facets of the curriculum to improve students' literacy development, their understanding of key content, and their motivation to learn. The sky is the limit—or, given the topic at hand, there's no telling where good reading instruction can take you!

Chapter 8

Assessing Word Recognition and Fluency Through Oral Reading

Effective Ways to Check Students' Progress

"The greatest teacher is not the one who talks all the time, but the one who listens."

—*Lauren, age 14*

Assessing reading is important. If you want to provide the best instruction for your students, you have to know their strengths and weaknesses. You have to know the level at which they are reading. And you have to track their progress to know whether your instruction is having an impact. This chapter looks at using oral reading to assess students' development in word recognition and fluency—two critical elements in overall reading success (National Reading Panel, 2000).

As Lauren points out in the opening quote, assessing is a form of listening or, shall we say, observing. How can we observe the act of reading? It's a difficult task because what happens during reading takes place primarily in the brain. Recent work by cognitive scientists using brain imaging technology has shown that certain areas of the brain become more active during reading (Wolfe, 2001). While these findings are interesting, they do not provide definitive recommendations for how best to teach reading.

In most cases, we don't assess during reading, but afterward. Consider standardized tests, for example: The student reads a series of passages silently and then answers a set of comprehension questions after each passage, usually by marking the correct answer on a list of choices. Or the student reads a passage or series of passages silently and writes a summary or other response after the reading. The student's achievement is determined by the number of questions he or she answers correctly or by the quality of a written response. The actual reading process, in these cases, is hidden within the reader.

Oral reading, however, offers us a window into the reading process. Strengths and weaknesses in word recognition, fluency, and, to a lesser extent, comprehension can be measured by analyzing the quality of the student's oral reading. We can even make inferences about the strategies the student is using based on the number and type of deviations he or she makes. In this chapter, I present simple, yet valid and effective, approaches for assessing various aspects of reading fluency through oral reading.

➤ Assessing Word Recognition (Decoding)

Successful reading demands a certain level of accuracy in decoding words. The standard to indicate adequate decoding while reading a continuous text is generally within the range of 92 to 98 percent accuracy (Gillet & Temple, 2000; Rasinski & Padak, 2005a, 2005b).

The 92 to 98 percent range is most commonly referred to as the instructional level: the point at which a student can read the text, but with the assistance of someone, usually a teacher. This is the level at which the reader is most likely to make the greatest progress in reading because the text is not too easy and not too difficult. A 99 to 100 percent level of accuracy generally indicates independent reading level for that text—the text can be read successfully without assistance. Word recognition below 92 percent is the marker for frustration level. If the reader makes more than 10 decoding errors for every 100 words, the text is most likely too difficult, even if assistance is provided.

Keep in mind that the word recognition scores you obtain need to be interpreted with care. A student may perform poorly on one reading because of a variety of factors other than his or her word recognition skills. The student may be having a bad day, feeling ill, or reading a passage that does not interest him or her. All assessments presented in this chapter require the expertise of a thoughtful educator to reflect upon and interpret them. That is why I recommend that if you feel uncomfortable with any assessment, you should administer it again, perhaps on another day. A major benefit of the assessments I present in this chapter is that they are so simple to administer and interpret and take so little time that they can be administered relatively often. The assessments are really a tool for the teacher to use to make professional judgments about a student's reading and make decisions on how best to help that student.

Reading Levels by Word Recognition Accuracy

Independent Level 99–100% accuracy
Student can read text independently without assistance.
Instructional Level 92–98% accuracy
Student can read text with instructional assistance.
Frustration Level Below 92% accuracy
Student had great difficulty reading the text, even
with assistance.

Informal Reading Inventories

A student's overall reading level can be determined with an informal reading inventory (IRI). There are many commercial IRIs available, and all of them have the same basic features: a leveled set of word lists and passages with comprehension questions. In an IRI, a student is asked to read orally a series of graded and progressively more difficult passages. The level at which the student reads with 92 to 98 percent accuracy, and with adequate comprehension, is his or her instructional level.

Consider this example: Tanya and Billy are fourth graders. For an IRI assessment, Tanya reads the third-grade passage at 99 percent word recognition accuracy and the fourth-grade passage at 96 percent accuracy. We consider her word recognition or decoding skills to be right where they should be, at grade 4.

Billy, however, reads the third- and fourth-grade passages with 94 percent and 88 percent word recognition accuracy, respectively. So Billy is at a third-grade instructional level, and a fourth-grade frustration level. In other words, he is one grade level behind in his word-recognition development.

One-Minute Reading Probe for Assessing Word Recognition

A complete IRI is time consuming to administer; it often takes an hour or more. However, there are other, faster methods to determine if a student is reading on grade level, such as the one-minute reading probe (Deno, 1985; Rasinski, 2004). When you administer reading probes regularly over time, they can help you determine whether your students are responding to word recognition instruction and making adequate progress.

To administer a one-minute reading probe, the teacher chooses a passage at the student's grade level, which the student has not seen before. (The grade level of the passage can be determined in a number of ways. See Figure 4.1 on page 94 for options.) After giving the student a brief introduction to the passage, the teacher asks the student to read orally for one minute, in a typical manner, using his or her best voice. While the student reads, the teacher follows along on a copy of the passage and marks any errors the reader makes, usually with a slash mark through the missed word. (See Figure 8.1 on page 184.) Errors include mispronunciations, substitutions, reversals, or omissions. If the text says one thing and the reader says another, or if the reader skips the word, it's counted

Figure 8.1

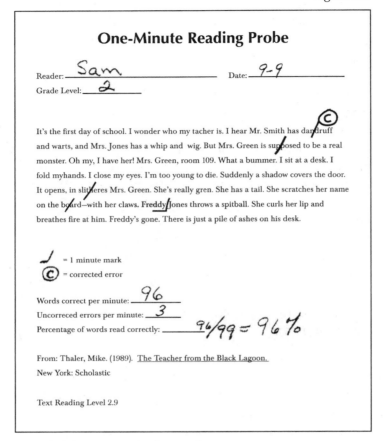

One-Minute Reading Probe

Reader: Sam   Date: 9-9

Grade Level: 2

It's the first day of school. I wonder who my tacher is. I hear Mr. Smith has dandruff and warts, and Mrs. Jones has a whip and wig. But Mrs. Green is supposed to be a real monster. Oh my, I have her! Mrs. Green, room 109. What a bummer. I sit at a desk. I fold myhands. I close my eyes. I'm too young to die. Suddenly a shadow covers the door. It opens, in slitheres Mrs. Green. She's really gren. She has a tail. She scratches her name on the board—with her claws. Freddy Jones throws a spitball. She curls her lip and breathes fire at him. Freddy's gone. There is just a pile of ashes on his desk.

= 1 minute mark

© = corrected error

Words correct per minute: 96

Uncorreced errors per minute: 3

Percentage of words read correctly: 96/99 = 96%

From: Thaler, Mike. (1989). The Teacher from the Black Lagoon. New York: Scholastic

Text Reading Level 2.9

A marked One-Minute Reading Probe passage

as an error. If the teacher gives the reader a word after a three-second pause, it's counted as an error as well. Repetitions are not counted as errors, though, nor are mispronunciations, substitutions, reversals, or omissions that the reader self-corrects. At the end of one minute, the teacher stops the student and marks that point in the text. (The teacher may also permit the student to complete the passage to bring closure to the reading experience.)

The percentage of accuracy is determined by dividing the number of words read correctly in the minute (WCPM) by the total number of words covered in the minute (TWPM). WCPM is determined by counting the total number of words read correctly to the one-minute mark on the passage. Total words covered in a minute is calculated by adding WCPM and the number of errors the student made. Let's take a look at some examples. To optimize the use of the one-minute reading probe, administer it three times to a student, using three different passages. Then use the average (mean) or middle (median) score from the three as the final score.

Tommy: An on-grade-level and developing reader

It's January, and Tommy, a new student, has just arrived in a third-grade class. His teacher wants to determine his level of word recognition proficiency on grade-level material. So she finds a third-grade passage that her students will be reading soon. During a quiet period, she asks Tommy to read the passage to her aloud for one minute. She marks his errors according to the guidelines above and obtains the following data:

WCPM: 104

Errors per minute: 4

TWPM: 108

Percent accuracy: 104/108 = 96.3% (rounded to 96%)

The 96 percent score indicates that Tommy decodes words in third-grade material at a level that is appropriate for third-grade students. His teacher may wish to perform this assessment one or two more times to ensure the reliability of the findings. And since the assessment requires only a minute or so to carry out, two or three more administrations shouldn't pose a difficulty.

Time that we give to reading assessment is usually time taken away from instruction. Whenever we can make quick assessments, without sacrificing reliability or validity, we can devote more time to teaching reading. The brevity of a reading probe also allows you time to give several assessments over the course of a school year in order to determine growth. So by administering reading probes to Tommy in March and June, his teacher will gain tangible evidence of his progress.

Here are Tommy's scores in word recognition accuracy on third-grade passages for that five-month period. With each administration, a new passage was given to Tommy. These passages are from the same book that contained the original passage:

January	**March**	**June**
96%	96%	99%

Indeed, the teacher provided herself with tangible evidence of Tommy's progress in word recognition.

Cynthia: A below-grade-level but developing reader

When they are used over time, one-minute reading probes help you document growth and identify areas of concern in students' reading. To illustrate this, let's look at third grader Cynthia's word recognition. In June, her teacher administered a reading probe using a third-grade passage and determined that she read with 90 percent accuracy. On the surface, it appears that Cynthia did not do well in her class because she ended the year decoding below a third-grade level. However, her teacher also administered probes to Cynthia at the beginning and middle of the year. Here is the data for the entire year:

September	January	June
84%	88%	90%

Although Cynthia is still not decoding text at a level that is commensurate with her grade placement, she has made great progress in her word recognition skills nonetheless. She has benefited from instruction. She is progressing. In a matter of minutes, Cynthia's teacher has her progress in decoding over an entire school year.

Peter: An on-grade-level but idle reader

Now consider Peter. Peter ends his third-grade year reading at a 95 percent level of accuracy on third-grade material. On the surface, it looks as if he has had a good year. However, looking at his performance over the school year reveals a somewhat different picture:

September	January	June
96%	95%	95%

Although Peter performed adequately in June, his yearlong performance indicates little growth in word recognition. Of course, his teacher would want to look at other factors that could impact growth in reading, such as school attendance, number of unfinished assignments, amount of reading done over the year, health problems, emotional problems in school or at home, and so on. However, this one indicator should signal some degree of concern. Certainly, Peter's fourth-grade teacher should be alerted to his lack of growth in third grade.

Refining the Analysis

The one-minute reading probe provides a quick snapshot of students' word recognition development. And for students who are developing along normal or expected lines, a quick snapshot may be all that you need—to verify what you already know. But what about those students who are performing significantly below grade level or are not growing as expected over the course of a school year? For these students, a deeper, more refined analysis is necessary to pinpoint specific areas of need and to address them through instruction.

Categorizing Errors by Type and Location

Identifying patterns of reading behavior by categorizing the type and location of word recognition errors will provide you with a more detailed picture of the child's strengths and weaknesses. Figure 8.2 below shows the way I sorted one student's errors. (A blank Word Recognition Error Form appears on page 188.) Categories of word recognition errors include mispronunciations, reversals, omissions, insertions, and refusals to attempt.

Figure 8.2

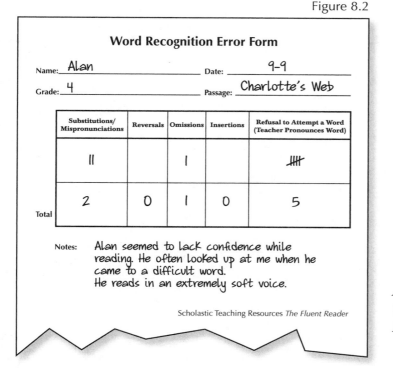

Word Recognition Error Form

Name: Alan   Date: 9-9

Grade: 4   Passage: Charlotte's Web

Substitutions/ Mispronunciations	Reversals	Omissions	Insertions	Refusal to Attempt a Word (Teacher Pronounces Word)
II		I		IIII
2	**0**	**1**	**0**	**5**

Total

Notes: Alan seemed to lack confidence while reading. He often looked up at me when he came to a difficult word.
He reads in an extremely soft voice.

Scholastic Teaching Resources *The Fluent Reader*

A completed Word Recognition Error Form

Figure 8.3

Word Recognition Error Form

Name: ______________________________ **Date:** ______________________

Grade: ______________________________ **Passage:** ______________________

	Substitutions/ Mispronunciations	Reversals	Omissions	Insertions	Refusal to Attempt a Word (Teacher Pronounces Word)
Total					

Notes:

Scholastic Teaching Resources *The Fluent Reader*

A significant percentage of errors in any of these categories may provide clues to the student's approach to decoding. For example:

- A student who has an unusually large number of refusals may be unwilling to try to figure out unknown words. Such a reader may benefit from instruction that builds his or her confidence and encourages the student to take risks when confronting unknown words.

- A student who regularly omits words while reading may read too quickly or carelessly and may benefit from instruction that encourages him or her to slow down and process the text more carefully.

- A student who often mispronounces words (e.g., *house* for *mouse* and *trouble* for *tremble*) may benefit from decoding instruction that focuses his or her attention on the sound-symbol patterns and relationships in words.

- A student who reverses letters within words (saying *saw* for *was*, and *mazagine* for *magazine*) beyond the primary grades may benefit from instruction that requires him or her to pay closer visual attention to the print while reading.

Listening to a recording of the reading with the student, and discussing errors with him or her, is a good way to confirm your inferences about the student's strengths and weaknesses. It's also a good way to make the student aware of the detrimental strategies that he or she may be using unconsciously. Researcher Yetta Goodman (1996) refers to this practice of reflecting on and talking about one's own reading performance and errors as "retrospective miscue analysis." By asking the student questions such as the following, we build his or her self-awareness as a reader:

- "What were you thinking about at this point in your reading?"
- "Does this error make sense in this passage?"
- "Does the word you said look like the one that is printed here?"
- "Do you think this error affected your understanding?"
- "Should you have corrected this error?"
- "How did you know to correct this error?"

Once students become aware of the kinds of errors they're making, and why they're making them, they can make conscious strides to overcome them. As Baker and Brown (1980) note, "If the child is aware of what is needed to perform effectively, then it is possible for him to take steps to meet the demands of a learning situation more effectively. If, however, the child is not aware of his own limitations as a learner or the complexity of the task at hand, then he can hardly be expected to take preventative actions in order to anticipate or recover from problems."

When a student mispronounces a word, he or she often mispronounces only a portion of it while decoding the rest of the word correctly. You can examine mispronunciations by determining the location of the error in the word. For example, when a reader says *fail* for *hail*, the error is localized at the beginning of the word. When a reader reads *blow* for *below*, he or she has decoded the beginning and end of the word correctly. The error lies in the middle of the word. And when a reader decodes *beginning* as *begins*, he or she is decoding the end of the word incorrectly.

Categorizing errors along these lines will help you plan instruction. Indeed, working with a child on beginning consonants or consonant blends will be of little help if the majority of his or her errors occurs at the end of words. You need a more refined analysis to determine the type and location of errors the student is making, and to plan instruction accordingly.

Categorizing Errors by Cueing Systems

Word recognition errors can also be categorized by the cueing system the student employs, or doesn't employ, while reading. Cueing systems include the semantic, the syntactic, and the grapho-phonic.

Semantic: The error retains the author's message.
Example: "Three houses [homes] burned throughout the night."
Reader says *homes* for *houses*.
Syntactic: The error fits grammatically within the overall text.
Example: "Three houses burned [burn] throughout the night."
Readers says *burn* for *burned*.
Grapho-phonic: The error resembles, in terms of letters and sounds, the actual word in the text.
Example: "Three houses [horses] burned throughout the night."
Reader says *horses* for *houses*.

By categorizing errors according to a cueing system and searching for patterns of errors, you can determine how the student approaches the words in the text. You'll discover whether he or she is using the letters and sounds in the unknown word, using knowledge of the way words fit grammatically into a sentence, or using the meaning the author is trying to convey. Identifying the cueing system a reader is using (or isn't using) can help you design instruction that corrects deficits and expands his or her ability to decode and read. Figure 8.4 on page 191 shows a completed form for analyzing locational errors (the location of the error within the word) and miscues (the type of error—sound-symbol or meaning). Figure 8.5 on page 192 provides a blank form for you to use.

Figure 8.4

Word Recognition Error Analysis Form

Reader: __Margaret__   Date: __9-10__

Reader	Text	Reader fails to use grapho-phonic information at this portion of the word			Final reading of error makes sense semantically and syntactically	
		Beginning	**Middle**	**End**	**Yes**	**No**
a	the	✔	✔	✔		✔
dollar	collar	✔				✔
dog	doggy			✔	✔	
leach	leash			✔		✔
mos	most			✔		✔
absolute	absolutely			✔		✔
hold	held		✔			✔
someone	somebody		✔	✔	✔	
Percentage of errors using:		Beginning-of-word information	Middle-of-word information	End-of-word information	Semantic and syntactic information	
		⁶/₈ 75%	⁵/₈ 63%	²/₈ 25%	²/₈ 25%	

Scholastic Teaching Resources   *The Fluent Reader*

A completed Word Recognition Error Analysis Form

➤ Assessing Fluency

Reading fluency is normally assessed through oral reading on the assumption that oral reading reflects, to some degree, the way we read silently.

Word Recognition Error Analysis Form

Figure 8.5

Reader:_____ Date:_____

Reader	Text	Reader fails to use grapho-phonic information at this portion of the word			Final reading of error makes sense semantically and syntactically	
		Beginning	Middle	End	Yes	No
Percentage of errors using:		Beginning-of-word information	Middle-of-word information	End-of-word information	Semantic and syntactic information	

Scholastic Teaching Resources   *The Fluent Reader*

Reading Rate

One way to assess fluency (automaticity in word recognition) is by measuring a student's reading rate—the number of words he or she reads correctly per minute. Figure 8.6 on page 193 shows typical reading rates for students in grades 1 through 8 across the school year. The fact that norms change not only between grade levels, but also within grade levels from fall to spring, suggests that reading rate is a dynamic measure of reading fluency and that students' reading fluency is responsive to the instruction we provide.

Using the One-Minute Reading Probe for Assessing Fluency

The more fluent reader is able to decode words effortlessly or automatically, as well as correctly. Automaticity in word recognition is measured through reading rate, so the one-minute reading probe described in Chapter 4 is an excellent tool for assessing fluency as well as word recognition. To refresh your memory, when administering a one-minute reading probe, choose a passage at the student's grade level, ask the student to read the passage orally, mark any errors he or she makes on a copy of the passage, and stop the student at the end of one minute. From there, count the number of words read correctly. Compare the words read correctly per minute with the appropriate grade and time of year norm from Figure 8.6. If the result is below or near the low end of the range of normal reading rates, then you may suspect that the student has not yet achieved an adequate level of fluency in his or her reading. If fluency is a concern, administer the probe several times over a few days to ensure that the results you get are reliable. (A student can also be disfluent if his or her reading is well above the range of normal reading rates, and it appears to you that the student is not reading for meaning.)

This is a very efficient form of assessment. In a matter of minutes, you obtain the data that allows you to get a general assessment of word recognition and fluency (Rasinski & Padak, 2005a, 2005b). You can administer the assessment several times a year to many students, thus providing yourself with documentation of growth, or lack of growth, in their reading. Let's look at the fluency performance of three students.

Figure 8.6

Normal Fluency Ranges as Measured by Words Correct Per Minute (WCPM)

Grade	Fall	Winter	Spring
1	—	—	30–90 wcpm
2	30–80	50–100	70–130
3	50–110	70–120	80–140
4	70–120	80–130	90–140
5	80–130	90–140	100–150
6	90–140	100–150	110–160
7	100–150	110–160	120–170
8	110–160	120–180	130–180

Adapted from the following sources:
Hasbrouck & Tindal (1992).
Hasbrouck & Tindal (2006).
Howe & Shinn (2001).
Rasinski & Padak (2005a).
Rasinski & Padak (2005b).

Mick: An on-grade-level and developing reader

Mick is a fourth grader. In a one-minute reading probe administered in September using fourth-grade material, he read 97 words correctly. The normal range for early fourth grade is 70–120 WCPM, so Mick began the year reading at grade level for fluency. Similar assessments done in January and June indicate that Mick is reading at 114 and 122 WCPM. His teacher should be quite happy with Mick's fluency performance because he not only made consistent gains throughout the school year, he also stayed within expectations for a fourth-grade student. His teacher's instruction had the desired effect.

Angela: A below-grade-level but developing reader

Angela, however, begins her fourth-grade year reading 68 WCPM on a fourth-grade passage, below grade-level expectations. Knowing this information helps her teacher develop instruction for Angela that focuses on reading fluency. In this particular case, the teacher chose to use the fluency development lesson (see Chapter 6). By January, Angela is able to read a fourth-grade passage at 105

WCPM, and by June, she is up to 125 WCPM. Angela made exceptional progress through the school year largely because her teacher used the information gained from the one-minute reading probe in September to tailor instruction that met her needs and accelerated her progress.

Kevin: An above-grade-level but idle reader

Kevin begins his fourth-grade year reading at an amazing 120 WCPM. So, naturally, his teacher expects great things from him based on this early assessment. However, in the January assessment, she notes that Kevin's fluency level has not improved. His score of 118 WCPM indicates that four months of instruction has not resulted in any improvement in reading fluency. With this information, Kevin's teacher decides to provide more opportunities for him to practice and perform his reading for classmates, which will hopefully improve his fluency. (See Chapters 4, 5, and 6 for examples of the types of instruction Kevin's teacher might use.)

The one-minute reading probe is a quick assessment that gives only a glimpse of a student's reading. Any concerns that the probe reveals should lead to more in-depth assessment of and consultation with the student. As I discussed earlier in the chapter, other factors may be at the root of a reading problem. Kevin's lack of growth in fluency, for example, may have been due to difficulties at home. Or it may have been due to the fact that he was reading more nonfiction material and needed to process the text in a more deliberate fashion to ensure comprehension. If that is the case, more instruction in fluency may not be good medicine. Rather, comprehension instruction may be more appropriate. Unless his teacher combines the assessment with student and/or parent conferences, misdiagnoses and inappropriate reading interventions may occur.

Questions to Ask in a Conference to Learn More About a Reader

- How would you describe yourself as a reader?
- Do you like to read? Why or why not?
- How often do you read for pleasure at home?
- Do you have a good place to read at home?

- Do you read for pleasure at school? What do you read for pleasure at school?
- What are you good at in reading?
- What are some areas you think you need to improve in your reading?
- When you come to a word you don't know in your reading, what do you do?
- Do you think you read too fast, too slow or just right for your grade level? Are you able to adjust the speed of your reading when you need to? How do you know when you need to read a bit slower? Faster?
- What do you do when you come to a passage that is difficult to read?
- What do you need to do to become a better reader?

Fluency (Prosody) Rubrics

Listening to students read and scoring their reading on a descriptive rubric or rating scale, where the focus is on reading with appropriate and meaningful expression (i.e., prosody), is another, more holistic way of assessing fluency. To administer a fluency rubric, record a student reading a couple of selected passages orally (normally the passages should be at the student's grade level placement and one grade level below). Then, when you have a quiet moment, listen to and rate the student's reading, according to the rating scale and descriptors in the rubric. A student who reads with appropriate fluency should score in the upper half of the rubric.

NAEP Fluency Scale

In studies of oral reading fluency sponsored by the United States Department of Education (Daane et al., 2005; Pinnell et al., 1995), researchers employed a four-point fluency rubric. (See Figure 8.7 on page 198 for a modified version.) Fourth graders were asked to read orally a brief passage they had previously practiced. Readings were then rated against the rubric.

Rubric scores enabled researchers to differentiate fourth graders' oral reading, even after they had practiced the text twice. Moreover, they found a significant correlation between rubric ratings and students' performance on a silent reading test. Students who scored highest on the rubric (levels 3 and 4) also scored highest on a silent reading comprehension test, and those with the lowest oral fluency rubric scores (levels 1 and 2) had the poorest comprehension when reading silently.

Multidimensional Fluency Scale

The adapted NAEP rubric is a simple, holistic scale. Because fluency is made up of a number of various features, such as expression and phrasing, Jerry Zutell and I (1991) developed the multidimensional fluency scale (MFS) for rating students' oral reading. An adaptation of the scale is presented in Figure 8.8 on page 199.

The MFS allows for greater precision in assessing specific areas of reading fluency. It allows you to narrow in on the aspect of fluency that needs greatest attention. Because the MFS has four subscales, you will probably need to listen to a reading several times and assess each dimension separately. The MFS is administered the same way the NAEP rubric is: You give students passages at and below their grade level, record the reading, and later compare the reading to the rubric's descriptors.

We also found that the MFS is an excellent tool for helping teachers develop an expert ear for fluency. When used regularly, the rubric promoted a sensitivity to the various and important features of fluency during oral reading.

➤ Concluding Thoughts

See a reading assessment in action on the DVD.

By functioning as a window into the reading process, oral reading allows you to gain a detailed picture of how students approach and deal with text. It is particularly useful for assessing word recognition and fluency—key elements of successful reading. And although word recognition and fluency are not comprehension, which is the goal of reading, they are necessary for comprehension. For many readers, problems in word recognition or fluency cause difficulties in comprehension and overall reading proficiency. So overcoming those problems often results in significant improvements in comprehension. Oral reading is the tool for assessing word recognition and fluency directly, and, indirectly, comprehension.

Figure 8.7

Adapted Version of
NAEP's* Oral Reading Fluency Scale

Level 1: Reads primarily in a word-by-word fashion. Occasional two-word and three-word phrases may occur, but these are infrequent. Author's meaningful syntax is generally not preserved. Passage is read without expression or intonation. Reading seems labored and difficult.

Note: A score of 1 can also be given to a student who reads in an excessively fast manner and appears to have little regard for reading with appropriate and meaningful expression.

Level 2: Reads primarily in two-word phrases with occasional three- or four-word phrases. Some word-by-word reading may be present. Word groupings may be awkward and unrelated to the larger context of the sentence or passage. Passage is read with little or inappropriate expression or intonation.

Level 3: Reads primarily in three- or four-word phrases. Some smaller phrases may be present. Most of the phrasing is appropriate and preserves the author's syntax. Some of the text is read with appropriate expression and intonation.

Level 4: Reads primarily in longer, meaningful phrases. Although some regressions, repetitions, and deviations from the text may be present, these do not appear to detract from the overall structure or meaning of the passage. The reading preserves the author's syntax. Most of the text is read with appropriate expression and intonation. A sense of ease is present in the reader's oral presentation.

Students should be asked to read passages at and below their assigned grade placement. Ratings of 3 and 4 indicate fluent reading. Ratings of 1 and 2 indicate that the student has still not achieved a minimal level of fluency for the grade level at which the passage is written.

* NAEP is an acronym for the National Assessment of Educational Progress, an ongoing program sponsored by the United States Department of Education that periodically evaluates students' educational achievement in a variety of curricular areas, including reading.

Multidimensional Fluency Scale

Figure 8.8

Use the following subscales to rate reader fluency on the four dimensions of expression and volume, phrasing, smoothness, and pace. Scores will range from 4 to 16. Scores of 9 and above indicate that fluency has been achieved for the grade level of the passage read. Scores at or below 8 indicate that fluency may be a concern. (You can record scores on the chart shown in Figure 8.9 on page 200.)

A. Expression and Volume

1. Reads with little expression or enthusiasm in voice. Reads words as if to simply get them out. Little sense of trying to make text sound like natural language. Tends to read in a quiet voice.
2. Some expression. Begins to use voice to make text sound like natural language in some areas of the text, but not others. Focus remains largely on saying the words. Still reads in a voice that is quiet.
3. Sounds like natural language throughout the better part of the passage. Occasionally slips into expressionless reading. Voice volume is generally appropriate throughout the text.
4. Reads with good expression and enthusiasm throughout the text. Sounds like natural language. Reader is able to vary expression and volume to match his/her interpretation of the passage.

B. Phrasing

1. Monotonic with little sense of phrase boundaries, frequent word-by-word reading; usually exhibits improper stress and intonation that fail to mark ends of sentences and clauses.
2. Frequent two- and three-word phrases giving the impression of choppy reading; often exhibits improper stress and intonation that fail to mark ends of sentences and clauses.
3. Mixture of run-ons, mid-sentence pauses for breath, and possibly some choppiness; reasonable stress/intonation.
4. Generally well-phrased, mostly in clause and sentence units, with adequate attention to expression.

C. Smoothness

1. Frequent extended pauses, hesitations, false starts, sound-outs, repetitions, and/or multiple attempts.
2. Several "rough spots" in text where extended pauses, hesitations, etc. are more frequent and disruptive.
3. Occasional breaks in smoothness caused by difficulties with specific words and/or structures.
4. Generally smooth reading with some breaks, but word and structure difficulties are resolved quickly, usually through self-correction.

D. Pace (during sections of minimal disruption)

1. Slow and laborious.
2. Moderately slow.
3. Uneven mixture of fast and slow reading.
4. Consistently conversational and appropriate for the nature of the text.

Figure 8.9

Multidimensional Fluency Scale Score Sheet

Reader:_____ Date:_____

Score	Expression & Volume	Phrasing	Smoothness	Pace

Scholastic Teaching Resources   *The Fluent Reader*

Bibliography of Professional Books and Articles

Allington, R. L. (1983). Fluency: The neglected goal of the reading program. *The Reading Teacher, 36*, 556–561.

Baker, L., & Brown, A. (1980). *Metacognitive skills and reading.* (Technical Report #18). Urbana, IL: University of Illinois, Center for the Study of Reading. (ERIC Document Reproduction Service No. ED195932).

Baum, R. The home schooling of Andrew Wyeth. *Gifted Child Monthly, 7*(5), 1–3, 13.

Bear, D. R., Invernizzi, M., Templeton, S., & Johnston, F. (1996). *Words their way: Word study for phonics, vocabulary, and spelling instruction.* Upper Saddle River, NJ: Merrill.

Beck, I. L., & McKeown, M. G. (2001). Text talk: Capturing the benefits of read-aloud experiences for young children. *The Reading Teacher, 55*, 10–20.

Biggs, M., Homan, S., Dedrick, R., Minick, V., & Rasinski, T. (2008). Using an interactive singing software program: A comparative study of middle school struggling readers. *Reading Psychology, 29*(3), 195–213.

Blachowicz, C., & Fisher, P. (2009). *Teaching vocabulary in all classrooms* (4th ed.). Boston: Allyn & Bacon.

Block, C. C., Parris, S. R., & Whiteley, C. S. (2008). CPMs: A kinesthetic comprehension strategy. *The Reading Teacher, 61*(6), 460–470.

Bromage, B. K., & Mayer, R. E. (1986). Quantitative and qualitative effects of repetition on learning from technical text. *Journal of Educational Psychology, 78*, 271–278.

Buswell, G. T., & Wheeler, W. H. (1923). *The silent reading hour: Teacher's manual for the third Reader.* Chicago: Wheeler Publishing.

Carbo, M. (1978a). Teaching reading with talking books. *The Reading Teacher, 32*, 267–273.

Carbo, M. (1978b). A word imprinting technique for children with severe memory disorders. *Teaching Exceptional Children, 11*, 3–5.

Carbo, M. (1981). Making books talk to children. *The Reading Teacher, 35*, 186–189.

Carver, R. P., & Hoffman, J. V. (1981). The effect of practice through repeated reading on gain in reading ability using a computer-based instructional system. *Reading Research Quarterly, 16*, 374–390.

Cazden, C. B. (1972). *Child language and education.* New York: Holt, Rinehart, Winston.

Chomsky, C. (1976). After decoding: What? *Language Arts, 53*, 288–296.

Cobb, L. (1835). *The North American reader.* New York: B. & S. Colins.

Cohen, D. (1968). The effect of literature on vocabulary and comprehension. *Elementary English, 45*, 209–213, 217.

Cunningham, A. E., & Stanovich, K. E. (1998). What reading does for the mind. *American Educator, 22*, 8–15.

Cunningham, P. M. (1995). *Phonics they use: Words for reading and writing* (2nd ed.). New York: HarperCollins.

Daane, M. C., Campbell, J. R., Grigg, W. S., Goodman, M. J., & Oranje, A. (2005). *Fourth-grade students reading aloud: NAEP 2002 special study of oral reading.* Washington, DC: U.S. Department of Education, Institute of Education Sciences.

Dahl, P. (1974). An experimental program for teaching high speed word recognition and comprehension skills (Final Report Project #3-1154). Washington, DC: National Institute of Education. (ERIC Document Reproduction Service No. ED 099 812).

Deno, S. L. (1985). Curriculum-based measurement: The emerging alternative. *Exceptional Children, 52,* 219–232.

Dowhower, S. L. (1987). Effects of repeated reading on second-grade transitional readers' fluency and comprehension. *Reading Research Quarterly, 22,* 389–406.

Dowhower, S. L. (1989). Repeated reading: Research into practice. *The Reading Teacher, 42,* 502–507.

Dowhower, S. L. (1994). Repeated reading revisited: Research into practice. *Reading and Writing Quarterly, 10,* 343–358.

Duke, N. K., Pressley, M., & Hilden, K. (2004). Difficulties with reading comprehension. In C. A. Stone, E. R. Silliman, B. J. Ehren, & K. Apel (Eds.), *Handbook of language and literacy: Development and disorders* (pp. 501–520). New York: Guilford.

Durkin, D. (1966). *Children who read early.* New York: Teachers College Press.

Edwards, Bob. (Interviewee). (2000). *Interview with NPR's Bob Edwards–October 2000.* Retrieved from JournalismJobs Web site: http://www.journalismjobs.com/interview_bobedwards.cfm.

Eldredge, J. L., Reutzel, D. R., & Hollingsworth, P. M. (1996). Comparing the effectiveness of two oral reading practices: Round-robin reading and the shared book experience. *Journal of Literacy Research, 28*(2), 201–225.

Faver, S. (2008). Repeated reading of poetry can enhance reading fluency. *The Reading Teacher, 62*(4), 350–352.

Fountas, I. C., & Pinnell, G. S. (1996). *Guided reading: Good first teaching for all children.* Portsmouth, NH: Heinemann.

Fountas, I. C., & Pinnell, G. S. (2001). *Guiding readers and writers, grades 3–6.* Portsmouth, NH: Heinemann.

Fry, E. B. (1980). The new instant word list. *The Reading Teacher, 34*(3), 284–289.

Fry, E., & Rasinski, T. (2007). *Increasing fluency with high frequency word phrases* (grades 1–6). Huntington Beach, CA: Shell Educational.

Gambrell, L., Kapinus, B., & Wilson, R. (1987). Using mental imagery and summarization to achieve independence in comprehension. *The Journal of Reading, 30,* 638–642.

Gardner, H. (1983). *Frames of mind.* New York: Basic Books Inc.

Gillet, J. W., & Temple, C. (2000). *Understanding reading problems* (5th ed.). New York: Longman.

Goodman, Y. (1996). Revaluing readers while readers revalue themselves: Retrospective miscue analysis. *The Reading Teacher, 49*, 600–609.

Greene, F. (1979). Radio reading. In C. Pennock (Ed.), *Reading comprehension at four linguistic levels* (pp. 104–107). Newark, DE: International Reading Association.

Griffith, L. W., & Rasinski, T. V. (2004). A focus on fluency: How one teacher incorporated fluency with her reading curriculum. *The Reading Teacher, 58*, 126–137.

Harris, A. J., & Sipay, E. R. (1990). *How to increase reading ability* (9th ed.). New York: Longman.

Harste, J., Short, C., & Burke, C. (1988). *Creating classrooms for authors.* Portsmouth, NH: Heinemann.

Hartman, D. K., & Hartman, J. A. (1993). Reading across texts: Expanding the role of the reader. *The Reading Teacher, 47*, 202–211.

Hasbrouck, J. E., Ihnot, C., & Rogers, G. (1999). Read naturally: A strategy to increase oral reading fluency. *Reading Research and Instruction, 39*, 27–37.

Hasbrouck, J. E., & Tindal, G. A. (1992). Curriculum-based oral reading fluency norms for students in grades 2 through 5. *Teaching Exceptional Children, 24*, 41–44.

Hasbrouck, J. E., & Tindal, G. A. (2006). Oral reading fluency norms: A valuable assessment tool for reading teachers. *The Reading Teacher, 59*(7), 636–644.

Heckelman, R. G. (1969). A neurological impress method of reading instruction. *Academic Therapy, 4*, 277–282.

Henderson, A. (1988). Parents are a school's best friend. *Phi Delta Kappan, 70*, 148–153.

Herman, P. A. (1985). The effect of repeated reading on reading rate, speech pauses, and word recognition accuracy. *Reading Research Quarterly, 20*, 553–564.

Hoffman, J.V. (1987). Rethinking the role of oral reading in basal instruction. *Elementary School Journal, 87*, 367–373.

Hoffman, J.V. (1991). Teacher and school effects in learning to read. In R. Barr, M. Kamil, P. Mosenthal, & P. D. Pearson, (Eds.), *Handbook of reading research* (Vol. 2, pp. 911–950). White Plains, NY: Longman.

Hoffman, J. V., & Crone, S. (1985). The oral recitation lesson: A research-derived strategy for reading in basal texts. In J. A. Niles & R. V. Lalik (Eds.), *Issues in literacy: A research perspective, 34th Yearbook of the National Reading Conference* (pp. 76–83). Rockfort, NY: National Reading Conference.

Hoffman, J. V., Roser, N. L., & Battle, J. (1993). Reading aloud in classrooms: From the modal toward a "model." *The Reading Teacher, 46*, 496–503.

Hoffman, J. V., & Segel, K. (1983). *Oral reading instruction: A century of controversy (1880–1980).* Paper presented at the annual meeting of the International Reading Association, Anaheim, CA. (ERIC Document Reproduction Service No. ED 237-239).

Hollingsworth, P. M. (1978). An experimental approach to the impress method of teaching reading. *The Reading Teacher, 31*(6), 624–626.

Howe, K. B., & Shinn, M. M. (2001). *Standard reading assessment passages (RAPS) for use in general outcome measurements: A manual describing development and technical features.* Eden Prairie, MN: Edformations.

Huck, C. S. (1977). Literature as the content of reading. *Theory into Practice, 16*, 363–371.

Huey, E. B. (1908). *The psychology and pedagogy of reading.* New York: Macmillan.

Hyatt, A. V. (1943). *The place of oral reading in the school program: Its history and development from 1880–1941.* New York: Teachers College, Columbia University.

Indianapolis Public Schools. (1902). *Course of study in reading.*

Ivey, G., & Broaddus, K. (2001). "Just plain reading": A survey of what makes students want to read in middle school classrooms. *Reading Research Quarterly, 36*, 350–371.

James, W. (1892). *Psychology.* New York: Holt.

Klinkenborg, V. (2009, May 16). Some thoughts on the lost art of reading aloud. *The New York Times.* Retrieved May 31, 2009, from http://www.nytimes.com/2009/05/16/opinion/16sat4.html.

Koskinen, P. S., & Blum, I. H. (1984). Repeated oral reading and acquisition of fluency. In J. A. Niles & L. A. Harris (Eds.), *Changing perspectives on research in reading/ language processing and instruction: Thirty-third yearbook of the National Reading Conference* (pp. 183–187). Rochester, NY: National Reading Conference.

Koskinen, P. S., & Blum, I. H. (1986). Paired repeated reading: A classroom strategy for developing fluent reading. *The Reading Teacher, 40*, 70–75.

Koskinen, P. S., Wilson, R. M., Gambrell, L. B., & Neuman, S. B. (1993). Captioned video and vocabulary learning: An innovative practice in literacy instruction. *The Reading Teacher, 47*(1), 36–43.

Koskinen, P. S., Blum, I. H. Bisson, S. A., Phillips, S. M., Creamer, T. S., & Baker, T. K. (1999). Shared reading, books, and audiotapes: Supporting diverse students in school and at home. *The Reading Teacher, 52*(5), 430–444.

Koskinen, P. S., Blum, I. H., Bisson, S. A., Phillips, S. M., Creamer, T. S., & Baker, T. K. (2000). Book access, shared reading, and audio models: The effects of supporting the literacy learning of linguistically diverse students in school and at home. *Journal of Educational Psychology, 92*(1), 23–36.

Koskinen, P. S., Bowen, C. T., Gambrell, L. B., Jensema, C. J., & Kane, K. W. (1997, March). *Captioned television and literacy development: Effects of home viewing on learning disabled students.* Paper presented at the annual meeting of the American Educational Research Association, Chicago, IL.

Kress, R. A., & Johnson, M. S. (1970). In A. J. Harris (Ed.), *Casebook on reading disability* (pp. 1–24). New York: David McKay.

Kuhn, M. R., Schwanenflugel, P. J., Morris, R. D., Morrow, L., Woo, D. G., Meisinger, E. B., Sevcik, R. P., Bradley, B. A., & Stahl, S. A. (2006). Teaching children to become fluent and automatic readers. *Journal of Literacy Research, 38*(4), 357–387.

Kuhn, M. R., & Stahl, S. A. (2000). *Fluency: A review of developmental and remedial practices.* Ann Arbor, MI: Center for the Improvement of Early Reading Achievement.

Kulich, L., Evanchan, G., & Sidorova, V. (in press). The impact of the fluency development lesson on the fluency and comprehension development of "at-risk" first grader readers. *Yearbook of the Association of Literacy Educators and Researchers.*

LaBerge, D., & Samuels, S. A. (1974). Toward a theory of automatic information processing in reading. *Cognitive Psychology, 6*, 293–323.

Limbrick, L., McNaughton, S., & Cameron, S. (1985). Peer power: Using peer tutoring to help low progress readers in primary and secondary schools. *Set: Research Information for Teachers, 2*, 22.

Mann, H. (1891). Second annual report of the secretary of the board of education–1838. In *Life and works of Horace Mann, II* (pp. 531–532). Boston: Lee and Shephard.

Martinez, M., & Roser, N. (1985). Read it again: The value of repeated readings during storytime. *The Reading Teacher, 38*, 782–786.

Martinez, M., Roser, N., & Strecker, S. (1999). "I never thought I could be a star": A readers theatre ticket to reading fluency. *The Reading Teacher, 52*, 326–334.

Mathes, P. G., Torgesen, J. K., & Allor, J. H. (2001). The effects of peer-assisted literacy strategies for first-grade readers with and without additional computer-assisted instruction in phonological awareness. *American Educational Research Journal, 38*, 371–410.

Mayer, R. E. (1983). Can you repeat that? Qualitative effects of repetition and advance organizers from science prose. *Journal of Educational Psychology, 75*, 40–49.

McDade, J. E. (1937). A hypothesis for non-oral reading: Argument, experiment, and results. *Journal of Educational Research, 30*, 489–503.

McDade, J. E. (1944). Examination of a recent criticism of non-oral beginning reading. *Elementary School Journal, 44*, 343–351.

McGuffey, W. H. (1879a). *McGuffey's second eclectic reader.* New York: American Book Company.

McGuffey, W. H. (1879b). *McGuffey's third eclectic reader.* New York: American Book Company.

McGuffey, W. H. (1887). *McGuffey's alternate first reader.* New York: American Book Company.

Morgan, R., & Lyon, E. (1979). Paired reading—A preliminary report on a technique for parental tuition of reading-retarded children. *Journal of Child Psychology and Psychiatry, 20*, 15–60.

Myers, C. A. (1978). Reviewing the literature on Fernald's technique of remedial reading. *The Reading Teacher, 31*, 614–619.

National Reading Panel. (2000). *Report of the National Reading Panel: Teaching children to read. Report of the subgroups.* Washington, DC: U.S. Department of Health and Human Services, National Institutes of Health.

Neill, K. (1980). Turn kids on with repeated reading. *Teaching Exceptional Children, 12*, 63–64.

Ness, M. (2009). Laughing through rereadings: Using joke books to build fluency. *The Reading Teacher, 62*(8), 691–694.

Neuman, S. B., & Koskinen, P. S. (1992). Captioned television as comprehensible input: Effects of incidental word learning in context for language minority students. *Reading Research Quarterly, 27*, 95–106.

Newell, M. A. (1880). *Newell's fourth reader.* Baltimore: John B. Piet and Co.

Nicholson, T. (1998). The flashcard strikes back. *The Reading Teacher, 52*, 188–192.

Opitz, M. F., & Rasinski, T. V. (2008). *Good-bye round robin: 25 effective oral reading strategies.* Portsmouth, NH: Heinemann.

O'Shea, L. J., & Sindelar, P. T. (1983). The effects of segmenting written discourse on the reading comprehension of low- and high-performance readers. *Reading Research Quarterly, 18*(4), 458–465.

Oster, L. (2001). Using the think-aloud for reading instruction. *The Reading Teacher, 55*, 64–69.

Padak, N., & Rasinski, T. (2003, April). *Family literacy programs: Who benefits?* Ohio Literacy Resource Center, Kent State University. Retrieved October 30, 2009. http://literacy.kent.edu/Oasis/Pubs/WhoBenefits2003.pdf.

Padak, N., & Rasinski, T. V. (2004). Fast Start: A promising practice for family literacy programs. *Family Literacy Forum, 3*, 3–9.

Padak, N., & Rasinski, T. (2005). *Fast Start for early readers.* New York: Scholastic.

Padak, N., & Rasinski, T. (2008). *Fast Start: Getting ready to read.* New York: Scholastic.

Paige, D. D. (2008). *An evaluation of whole-class choral reading using science text on oral reading fluency in struggling adolescents.* Unpublished doctoral dissertation, University of Memphis.

Paige, D. D. (2009). *What can we do for struggling readers?: Whole-class choral reading as a middle school fluency strategy.* Unpublished manuscript.

Parker, F. W. (1884). *Talks on pedagogics.* New York: Barnes and Co.

Perfect, K. A. (1999). Rhyme and reason: Poetry for the heart and head. *The Reading Teacher, 52*, 728–737.

Perfect, K. A. (2005). *Poetry lessons: Everything you need: A mentor teacher's lessons and select poems that help you meet the standards across the curriculum—and teach poetry with confidence and joy.* New York: Scholastic.

Person, M. (1990). Say it right! *The Reading Teacher, 43*, 428–429.

Piaget, J., & Inhelder, B. (1969). *The psychology of the child.* New York: Basic Books.

Pinnell, G. S., Pikulski, J. J., Wixson, K. K., Campbell, J. R., Gough, P. B., & Beatty, A. S. (1995). *Listening to children read aloud.* Washington, DC: Office of Educational Research and Improvement, U. S. Department of Education.

Pinsky, R. (October 20, 2006). *The Writer's Almanac.* Retrieved from http://writersalmanac.publicradio.org/index.php?date=2006/10/20.

Postlethwaite, T. N., & Ross, K. N. (1992). *Effective schools in reading: Implications for policy planners.* The Hague: International Association for the Evaluation of Educational Achievement.

Rashotte, C. A., & Torgeson, J. K. (1985). Repeated reading and reading fluency in learning-disabled children. *Reading Research Quarterly, 20,* 180–188.

Rasinski, T.V. (1990). *The effects of cued phrase boundaries in texts.* Bloomington, IN: ERIC Clearinghouse on Reading and Communication Skills (ED 313 689).

Rasinski, T.V. (1994). Developing syntactic sensitivity in reading through phrase-cued texts. *Intervention in School and Clinic, 29,* 165–168.

Rasinski, T. V. (1995). Fast Start: A parental involvement reading program for primary grade students. In W. Linek & E. Sturtevant (Eds.), *Generations of literacy: Seventeenth Yearbook of the College Reading Association* (pp. 301–312). Harrisonburg, VA: College Reading Association.

Rasinski, T. V. (2000). Speed does matter in reading. *The Reading Teacher, 54,* 146–151.

Rasinski, T. V. (2002). *Evaluation of the OSTI auditory feedback system for improving reading.* Unpublished manuscript.

Rasinski, T. V. (2004). *Assessing reading fluency.* Honolulu: Pacific Resources for Education and Learning. Available at www.prel.org/products/re_/assessing-fluency.pdf.

Rasinski, T. V. (2006). Reading fluency instruction: Moving beyond accuracy, automaticity, and prosody. *The Reading Teacher, 59,* 704–706.

Rasinski, T., Flexer, C., & Boomgarden-Szypulski, T. (2006). *The sound of learning: Why self-amplification matters.* Minneapolis: Harebrain.

Rasinski, T. V., & Fredericks, A. D. (1991). The Akron paired reading project. *The Reading Teacher, 44,* 514–515.

Rasinski, T. V., & Hoffman, J. V. (2003). Theory and research into practice: Oral reading in the school literacy curriculum. *Reading Research Quarterly, 38,* 510–522.

Rasinski, T. V., & Padak, N. D. (1998). How elementary students referred for compensatory reading instruction perform on school-based measures of word recognition, fluency, and comprehension. *Reading Psychology: An International Quarterly, 19,* 185–216.

Rasinski, T. V., & Padak, N. (2000). *Effective reading strategies: Teaching children who find reading difficult* (2nd Ed.). Columbus, OH: Merrill/Prentice Hall.

Rasinski, T., & Padak, N. (2005a). *Three-minute reading assessments: Word recognition, fluency, and comprehension* (Gr. 1–4). New York: Scholastic.

Rasinski, T., & Padak, N. (2005b). *Three-minute reading assessments: Word recognition, fluency, and comprehension* (Gr. 5–8). New York: Scholastic.

Rasinski, T. V., & Padak, N. D. (2008). *From phonics to fluency: Effective teaching of decoding and reading fluency in the elementary school (2nd ed.).* New York: Longman.

Rasinski, T. V., Padak, N., Linek, W., & Sturtevant, E. (1994). The effects of fluency development instruction on urban second grade readers. *Journal of Educational Research, 87,* 158–164.

Rasinski, T., Reutzel, D. R., Chard, D., & Linan-Thompson, S. (in press). Reading fluency. In M. Kamil, P. D. Pearson, P. Afflerbach, & E. B. Moje. (Eds.), *Handbook of reading research, Vol. IV.* New York: Routledge.

Rasinski, T., Rikli, A., & Johnston, S. (2009). Reading fluency: More than automaticity? More than a concern for the primary grades? *Literacy Research and Instruction, 48,* 350–361.

Rasinski, T., Rupley, W. H., Nichols, & W. D. (2008). Two essential ingredients: Phonics and fluency getting to know each other. *The Reading Teacher, 62*(3), 257–260.

Rasinski, T., Samuels, S. J., Hiebert, E., Petscher, Y., & Feller, K. (in press). The relationship between a silent reading fluency instructional protocol on students' reading comprehension and achievement in an urban school setting. *Reading Psychology: An International Quarterly.*

Rasinski, T., & Stevenson, B. (2005). The effects of Fast Start reading: A fluency based home involvement reading program, on the reading achievement of beginning readers. *Reading Psychology: An International Quarterly, 26*(2), 109–125.

Rasinski, T. V., & Zutell, J. B. (1996). Is fluency yet a goal of the reading curriculum? In E. G. Sturtevant and W. M. Linek (Eds.), *Growing literacy: 18th yearbook of the College Reading Association* (pp. 237–246). Harrisonburg, VA: College Reading Association.

Reutzel, D. R., & Hollingsworth, P. M. (1993). Effects of fluency training on second graders' reading comprehension. *Journal of Educational Research, 86,* 325–331.

Reutzel, D. R., Hollingsworth, P. M., & Eldredge, L. (1994). Oral reading instruction: The impact on student reading comprehension. *Reading Research Quarterly, 29,* 40–62.

Reutzel, D. R., Jones, C. D., Fawson, P. C., & Smith, J. A. (2008). Scaffolded silent reading: A complement to guided repeated oral reading that works! *The Reading Teacher, 62*(3), 194–207.

Rohrer, J. H. (1943). An analysis and evaluation of the "non-oral" method of reading instruction. *Elementary School Journal, 43,* 415–421.

Rosenblatt, L. M. (1978). *The reader, the text, the poem: The transactional theory of literary work.* Carbondale, IL: Southern Illinois University Press.

Samuels, S. J. (1979). The method of repeated reading. *The Reading Teacher, 32,* 403–408.

Schreiber, P. A. (1980). On the acquisition of reading fluency. *Journal of Reading Behavior, 12,* 177–186.

Schreiber, P. A. (1987). Prosody and structure in children's syntactic processing. In R. Horowitz & S. J. Samuels (Eds.), *Comprehending oral and written language* (pp. 243–270). New York: Academic Press.

Schreiber, P. A. (1991). Understanding prosody's role in reading acquisition. *Theory into Practice, 30*, 158–164.

Schreiber, P.A., & Read, C. (1980). Children's use of phonetic cues in spelling, parsing, and—maybe—reading. *Bulletin of the Orton Society, 30*, 209–224.

Searfoss, L. (1975). Radio reading. *The Reading Teacher, 29*, 295–296.

Sindelar, P. T., Monda, L. E., & O'Shea, L. J. (1990). Effects of repeated readings on instructional- and mastery-level readers. *Journal of Educational Research, 83*, 220–226.

Smith, J. W. A., & Elley, W. B. (1997). *How children learn to read.* Katonah, NY: Richard C. Owen.

Smith, N. B. (1965). *American reading instruction.* Newark, DE: International Reading Association.

Stahl, S. A., & Heubach, K. M. (2005). Fluency-oriented reading instruction. *Journal of Literacy Research, 37*(1), 25–60.

State of Ohio, Department of Education. (1923). Reading: A manual of suggestions for the use of the elementary schools in Ohio (Course of study series). Columbus: Heer Printing Co.

Stauffer, R. (1980). *The language experience approach to the teaching of reading.* New York: Harper & Row.

Steele, Sir Richard. (1709–1710). From my own apartment, March 17. *Tatler,* 147.

Strecker, S., Roser, N., & Martinez, N. (1998). Toward understanding oral reading fluency. In T. Shanahan & F. Rodriguez-Brown (Eds.), *Forty-seventh yearbook of the National Reading Conference* (pp. 295–310). Chicago: National Reading Conference.

Tan, A., & Nicholson, T. (1997). Flashcards revisited: Training poor readers to read words faster improves their comprehension of text. *Journal of Educational Psychology, 89*, 276–288.

Therrien, W. J. (2004). Fluency and comprehension gains as a result of repeated reading: A meta-analysis. *Remedial and Special Education, 25*(4), 252–261.

Topping, K. (1987a). Paired reading: A powerful technique for parent use. *The Reading Teacher, 40*, 604–614.

Topping, K. (1987b). Peer tutored paired reading: Outcome data from ten projects. *Educational Psychology, 7*, 133–145.

Topping, K. (1989). Peer tutoring and paired reading: Combining two powerful techniques. *The Reading Teacher, 42*(7), 488–494.

Topping, K. (1995). *Paired reading, spelling, and writing.* New York: Cassell.

Tower, D. B. (1871). *Tower's third reader.* Baltimore: Kelly, Piet, & Co.

Trelease, J. (2006). *The read-aloud handbook* (6th ed.). New York: Penguin.

Vacca, J. L., Vacca, R. T., & Gove, M. K. (2000). *Reading and learning to read* (4th ed.). New York: Longman.

Vaughn, S. (2000). Fluency and comprehension interventions for third-grade students. *Remedial and Special Education, 21*(6), 325–335.

Washburn, M. F. (1914). The function of incipient motor processes. *Psychological Review, 21*, 376–390.

Welty, E. (1998). *One writer's beginnings.* Cambridge, MA: Harvard University Press.

Wilhelm, J. D. (2002). *Action strategies for deepening comprehension.* New York: Scholastic.

Willingham, D. (2007). The usefulness of brief instruction in reading comprehension strategies. *American Educator, 30*, 39–45, 50.

Wolfe, P. (2001). *Brain matters: Translating research into classroom practice.* Alexandria, VA: Association for Supervision and Curriculum Development.

Worthy, J., & Broaddus, K. (2001/2002). Fluency beyond the primary grades: From group performance to silent, independent reading. *The Reading Teacher, 55*, 334–343.

Young, C., & Rasinski, T. (2009). Implementing readers theatre as an approach to classroom fluency instruction. *The Reading Teacher, 63*(1), 4–13.

Zull, J. E. (2002). *The art of changing the brain.* Sterling, VA: Stylus.

Zutell, J., & Rasinski, T. V. (1991). Training teachers to attend to their students' oral reading fluency. *Theory into Practice, 30*, 211–217.

Bibliography of Children's Books

Hopkins, L. B. (Ed.). (1990). *Good books, good times!* New York: HarperCollins and Trumpet Book Club.

Larrick, N. (Ed.). (1990). *Mice are nice.* New York: Philomel.

Munsch, R. M. (1986). *Love you forever.* Buffalo, NY: Firefly Books.

Munsch, R. M. (1980). *The paper bag princess.* Toronto, Canada: Annick Press.

Rathmann, P. (1995). *Officer Buckle and Gloria.* New York: Putnam.

Service, R. (1940). *Collected poems of Robert Service.* New York: G. P. Putnam's Sons.

Silverstein, S. (1974). *Where the sidewalk ends.* New York: HarperCollins.

Taylor, M. D. (1976). *Roll of thunder, hear my cry.* New York: Dial.

Van Allsburg, C. (1990). *Just a dream.* Boston: Houghton Mifflin.

Viorst, J. (1972). *Alexander and the terrible, horrible, no good, very bad day.* New York: Atheneum.

Appendix:
Texts for Practice and Performance

Sojourner Truth and the Struggle for People's Equality
adapted by Timothy Rasinski

Parts: *Narrators 1–4* (can be combined), *Sojourner Truth*

Narrator 1: Long before the civil rights movement of the 1950s and '60s, in which certain Americans demanded that all citizens, regardless of the color of their skin, be treated fairly and with respect . . .

Narrator 2: Indeed, long before the women's rights movement of the 1960s and '70s, in which women demanded their right to be treated justly and with dignity . . .

Narrator 3: Even years before the start of the Civil War, a war fought to end slavery in the United States . . .

Narrator 4: There were people who spoke up for the rights of black people and the rights of women. One of those people was—

Narrators 1–4: Sojourner Truth.

Narrator 1: Sojourner Truth was a black woman, a Negro, and she was born into slavery in 1797.

Narrator 2: But Sojourner Truth was not afraid to speak out for what she thought was right and what she knew was wrong.

Narrator 3: In the years before the Civil War, Sojourner spoke throughout the northern and midwestern United States, to whoever would listen to her, about the evils of slavery and the need for all Americans to have equal rights.

Narrator 4: She was a powerful speaker. And since she stood six feet tall, people listened to what she had to say!

Narrator 1: In the 1850s, women in the United States did not have the same rights as men. They could not vote, they could not go to college, they could not own their own property.

Narrator 2: In many ways, women were the property of their husbands—almost like slaves themselves. Men did not think women were strong enough or smart enough to have the same rights as men.

Narrator 3: Many men thought that women were weak, that they needed to be helped into carriages, that they needed to be carried over ditches, that they needed to be taken care of by men.

Narrator 4: Besides, since Jesus Christ was a man, many men felt that that must be proof that men were superior to women and that women did not deserve the same rights as men.

Narrator 1: Women knew that this was not right and they began to speak out about this blatant unfairness.

Narrator 2: They began to organize meetings in which they spoke out about their lack of rights—

Narrator 3: But these meetings were run by white women, mostly from the northern states. Black women were neither welcome nor wanted.

Narrator 4: In 1851, a women's rights convention was held in Akron, Ohio. Many women and men spoke about the rights of women—white women, that is.

Narrator 1: But, in the middle of the convention, a tall black woman stood up and demanded to speak. Those at the meeting tried to keep her from speaking. They protested her presence loudly, and they demanded that she leave.

Narrator 2: This is a meeting for whites only! Get her out of here!

Narrator 3: No blacks allowed here!

Narrator 4: Let her speak to her own people. Make her leave.

Narrator 1: Sojourner Truth was not only tall, she was strong in her beliefs. She made her way to the podium, faced the group of angry white people, waited a few seconds . . . and told everyone that the struggle for the rights of white women was the struggle for all women, regardless of the color of their skin.

Sojourner: Well, children, where there is so much racket there must be something out of kilter. I think that between the Negroes of the South and the women of the North, all talking about rights, the white men will be in a fix pretty soon. But what's all this here talking about? That man over there says that women need to be helped into carriages, and lifted over ditches, and to have the best of everything. Nobody ever helps me into carriages, or over mud puddles, or gives me the best of anything! And ain't I a woman? Look at me! Look at my arm. I have plowed and planted, and gathered into barns, and no man could head me! And ain't I a woman? I could work as much and eat as much as a man—when I could get it—and I could bear the lash as well! And ain't I a woman? I have borne thirteen children, and have seen most all of them sold off to slavery, and when I cried out with my mother's grief, none but Jesus heard me! And ain't I a woman?

Narrator 2: By now the crowd was hushed. Sojourner's strong voice presided over the crowd. A silence descended on the audience. Heads began to nod in response to Sojourner's repeated question—Ain't I a woman?

Sojourner: Then they talk about this thing in the head; what's this they call it?

Narrator 3: You mean intellect?

Sojourner: That's it, honey. What's that got to do with women's rights or Negroes' rights? If my cup won't hold but a pint, and yours holds a quart, wouldn't you be mean not to let me have my little half-measure? Then that little man in black over there, he says that women can't have as much rights as men, cause Christ wasn't a woman! Where did your Christ come from? Where did your Christ come from? From God and a woman! Man had nothing to do with it. If the first woman God ever made was strong enough to turn the world upside down all alone, these women together ought to be able to turn it back, and get it right side up again! And now that they is asking to do it, the men better let them.

Obliged to you for hearing me, and now old Sojourner ain't got nothing more to say.

SILENCE FOR A FEW SECONDS

Narrator 4:   And with that, Sojourner Truth's speech was over. She left the podium, and she walked out of the meeting and into history. Yet her words still ring true today as they did on that day in 1851 . . .

Narrator 1:   Ain't I a woman?

Narrator 2:   Even though the color of my skin may be different from yours, inside we are all the same.

Narrator 3:   And I too deserve to be treated with equality, respect, and dignity.

The Night Before Christmas

by Clement C. Moore

To be performed by two readers: Reader 1 reads the left column of text. Reader 2 reads the right column, and both readers read the center column of boldface text together.

'Twas the night before Christmas, when all through the house
Not a creature was stirring, not even a mouse;

> The stockings were hung by the chimney with care,
> In hopes that St. Nicholas soon would be there.

The children were nestled all snug in their bed,
While visions of sugarplums danced in their heads;

> And mamma in her 'kerchief, and I in my cap,
> Had just settled our brains for a long winter's nap . . .

When out on the lawn there arose such a clatter,
I sprang from the bed to see what was the matter.

> Away to the window I flew like a flash,
> Tore open the shutters and threw up the sash.

The moon on the breast of the new-fallen snow
Gave the luster of mid-day to objects below,

> When, what to my wondering eyes should appear,

But a miniature sleigh, and eight tiny reindeer,

With a little old driver so lively and quick,

I knew in a moment it must be St. Nick.

> More rapid than eagles his coursers they came,
> And he whistled, and shouted, and called them
> by name:

"Now, Dasher! Now, Dancer! Now, Prancer and Vixen!

On, Comet!

On, Cupid!

On, Donder!

And Blitzen!

To the top of the porch! To the top of the wall!

Now, dash away! Dash away! Dash away all!"

As dry leaves that before the wild hurricane fly,

When they meet with an obstacle, mount to the sky,

So up to the house-top the coursers they flew,

With the sleigh full of toys, and St. Nicholas, too.

And then, in a twinkling, I heard on the roof

The prancing and pawing of each little hoof.

As I drew in my head, and was turning around,

Down the chimney St. Nicholas came with a bound.

He was dressed all in fur,

From his head to his foot,

And his clothes were all tarnished

With ashes and soot. A bundle of toys

He had flung on his back,

And he looked like a peddler

Just opening his pack.

His eyes—how they twinkled—his dimples how merry!
His cheeks were like roses, his nose like a cherry!

His droll little mouth was drawn up like a bow,
And the beard of his chin was as white as
the snow.

The stump of a pipe he held tight in his teeth,
And the smoke it encircled his head like a wreath.

He had a broad face and a little round belly
That shook, when he laughed, like a bowl full
of jelly.

He was chubby and plump, a right jolly old elf,

And I laughed when I saw him, in spite of myself.
A wink of his eye and a twist of his head

Soon gave me to know I had nothing to dread.
He spoke not a word, but went straight to his work,

And filled all the stockings; then turned with a jerk,
And laying his finger aside of his nose,

And giving a nod, up the chimney he rose.
He sprang to his sleigh, to his teams gave a whistle,

And away they all flew like the down of a thistle.
But I heard him exclaim, ere he drove out of sight,
"Happy Christmas to all, and to all a good-night!"

The Three Billy Goats Gruff (With Attitude!)

Adapted by Timothy Rasinski
With Second Graders From Kent State University's Reading Clinic

Parts: *Little Billy Goat Gruff, Middle-Size Billy Goat Gruff, Big Billy Goat Gruff, Troll, Narrators 1 and 2*

Narrator 1: Welcome to our show. Today's play is "The Three Billy Goats Gruff (With Attitude!)"

Little BGG: "I'm Little Billy Goat Gruff!"

Middle BGG: "I'm Middle-Size Billy Goat Gruff!"

Big BGG: "Hello there, I'm Big Billy Goat Gruff!"

Troll: "Do you know who I am? I'm the Troll—and today I am very, very hungry! Grrrrr!"

Narrator 2: As Little Billy Goat Gruff strolls through the fields, he sees a rickety, old bridge. On the other side of the bridge is a meadow with green, green grass and apple trees filled with red, red apples.

Little BGG: "I'm the littlest billy goat. I have two big brothers. I want to go across this bridge to eat some green, green grass and red, red apples so that I can be big like my two brothers."

Narrator 1: And so, Little Billy Goat Gruff starts across the bridge.

All *(softly)*: Trip, trap, trip, trap, trip, trap.

Narrator 2: Just as Little Billy Goat Gruff comes to the middle of the bridge, an old troll pops up from underneath it.

Troll: "Who is that walking on my bridge? Snort! Snort!"

Little BGG: "It's only me, Little Billy Goat Gruff."

Troll:	"Arrrgh! I'm a big, bad troll, and you are on my bridge. I'm going to eat you for my breakfast. Snort! Snort!"
Little BGG:	"I just want to eat some green, green grass and red, red apples in the meadow. Please don't eat me, Mister Troll. I'm just a little billy goat. Wait until my brother comes along. He is much bigger and tastier than me."
Troll:	"Bigger? Tastier? Well, alright. I guess I will. Go ahead and cross the bridge. Arrrgh!"
Little BGG:	"Thank you very much, you great big, ugly, old troll."
Troll:	"What did you call me? Come back here! Grrrr!"
Little BGG:	"Bye!"
All *(softly)*:	Trip, trap, trip, trap, trip, trap.
Narrator 1:	Little Billy Goat Gruff runs across the bridge. He eats the green, green grass and red, red apples. The troll goes back under his bridge and falls asleep.
Narrator 2:	Before long, Middle-Size Billy Goat Gruff walks up to the rickety, old bridge. He, too, sees the meadow with the green, green grass and apple trees filled with red, red apples.
Middle BGG:	"I'm the middle-size billy goat. I have a big brother and a little brother. I want to go across this bridge to eat some green, green grass and red, red apples so that I can be big like my brother."
Narrator 1:	Middle-Size Billy Goat Gruff starts across the bridge.
All *(a bit louder, as Middle BGG is bigger)*:	Trip, trap, trip, trap, trip, trap.
Narrator 2:	Just as Middle-Size Billy Goat Gruff comes to the middle of the bridge, the old troll pops up from under the bridge.
Troll:	"Grrr! Who is that walking on my bridge? Arrrgh!"
Middle BGG:	"It is I, Middle-Size Billy Goat Gruff."

Troll: "Grrrr! I'm a big, bad troll, and you are on my bridge. I'm going to eat you for my lunch. Snort! Snort!"

Middle BGG: "I just want to eat some of that green, green grass and red, red apples in the meadow. Please don't eat me, Mister Troll. I'm just a middle-size billy goat. Wait until my brother comes along. He is much bigger and much, much tastier than I am."

Troll: "Bigger? Tastier? Hmmmmm. Alright, I guess I will. Go ahead and cross the bridge."

Middle BGG: "Thank you very much, you great big, really ugly, smelly, slimy, and dirty old troll."

Troll: "What did you call me? Grrrr! Come back here right this very instant!"

Middle BGG: "Oh, nothing. See ya!"

All *(a bit louder):* Trip, trap, trip, trap, trip, trap.

Narrator 1: Middle-Size Billy Goat Gruff runs across the bridge. He eats the green, green grass and the red, red apples. The troll goes back under his bridge and once again falls fast sleep.

Narrator 2: After a while, Big Billy Goat Gruff sees the rickety, old bridge. He also sees his two brothers on the other side of the bridge in the meadow eating the green, green grass and the red, red apples from the apple tree.

Big BGG: "I'm the biggest billy goat. I have two brothers. I want to go across this bridge to eat some green, green grass and red, red apples just as they did."

Narrator 1: Big Billy Goat Gruff starts across the bridge.

All *(louder this time):* Trip, trap, trip, trap, trip, trap.

Narrator 2: Just as Big Billy Goat Gruff gets to the middle of the bridge, the old troll pops up from under the bridge.

Troll: "Grrrr! Who is that walking on my bridge?"

Big BGG: "It is I, Big Billy Goat Gruff."

Troll: "Grrrr! I'm a big, bad troll and you are on my bridge. I'm going to eat you for my supper. Snort! Snort! Snort!"

Big BGG: "Really?" (smiles at the audience) "Well, then, Mr. Troll, come right on up here and have a feast." (smiles at the audience again)

Narrator 1: The troll climbs onto the bridge. Big Billy Goat Gruff lowers his head and charges the troll!

Big BGG: "Garrummmp!"

Narrator 2: Big Billy Goat Gruff knocks the troll clean off the bridge and into the icy cold water!

Troll: "Glug. Glug. Glug. Grrrrr. Grrrrr. Shiver. Shiver. Brrrrrr."

Big BGG: "Brothers, that ugly old bully won't bother us again. I butted him with my horns and knocked him off the bridge and into the icy cold water. I've done my job, and from now on we can come and go in peace. Now, I'm going to go and eat some of that green, green grass and some red, red apples."

All *(very loudly):* Trip, trap, trip, trap, trip, trap.

Narrator 2: Big Billy Goat Gruff crosses the bridge and joins his brothers. In the meadow, the three billy goats eat the green, green grass and red, red apples.

Big Billy Goat: "Munch, munch, munch."

Little and Middle-Size Billy Goats: "Munch, munch, munch."

All Three Billy Goats: "Munch, munch, munch. This green green grass is great for lunch!"

Narrator 1: What happened to that mean, ugly, old troll? He never came back to the bridge. He learned that being mean never pays.

Troll: "This water feels like ice. Brrr, brrr, brrr! Next time, I guess I'll try being nice!"

All: The End.

Index